The Dave Walker Colouring Book

Also by Dave Walker and available from Canterbury Press

Heroes of the Coffee Rota

Peculiar Goings On

The Exciting World of Churchgoing

The Dave Walker Guide to the Church

My Pew: Things I have Seen from it

www.canterburypress.co.uk

The Dave Walker Colouring Book

Dave Walker

CANTERBURY
PRESS
Norwich

© Dave Walker 2016

First published in 2016 by the Canterbury Press Norwich
Editorial office
3rd Floor, Invicta House,
108-114 Golden Lane,
London EC1Y 0TG.

Canterbury Press is an imprint of
Hymns Ancient & Modern (a registered charity)
13A Hellesdon Park Road, Norwich,
Norfolk, NR6 5DR,UK.

www.canterburypress.co.uk

British Library Cataloguing in Publication data

A catalogue record for this book is available
from the British Library

978 1 84825 897 6

Printed and bound in Great Britain by
CPI Group (UK) Ltd, Croydon

FOUND IN CHURCH

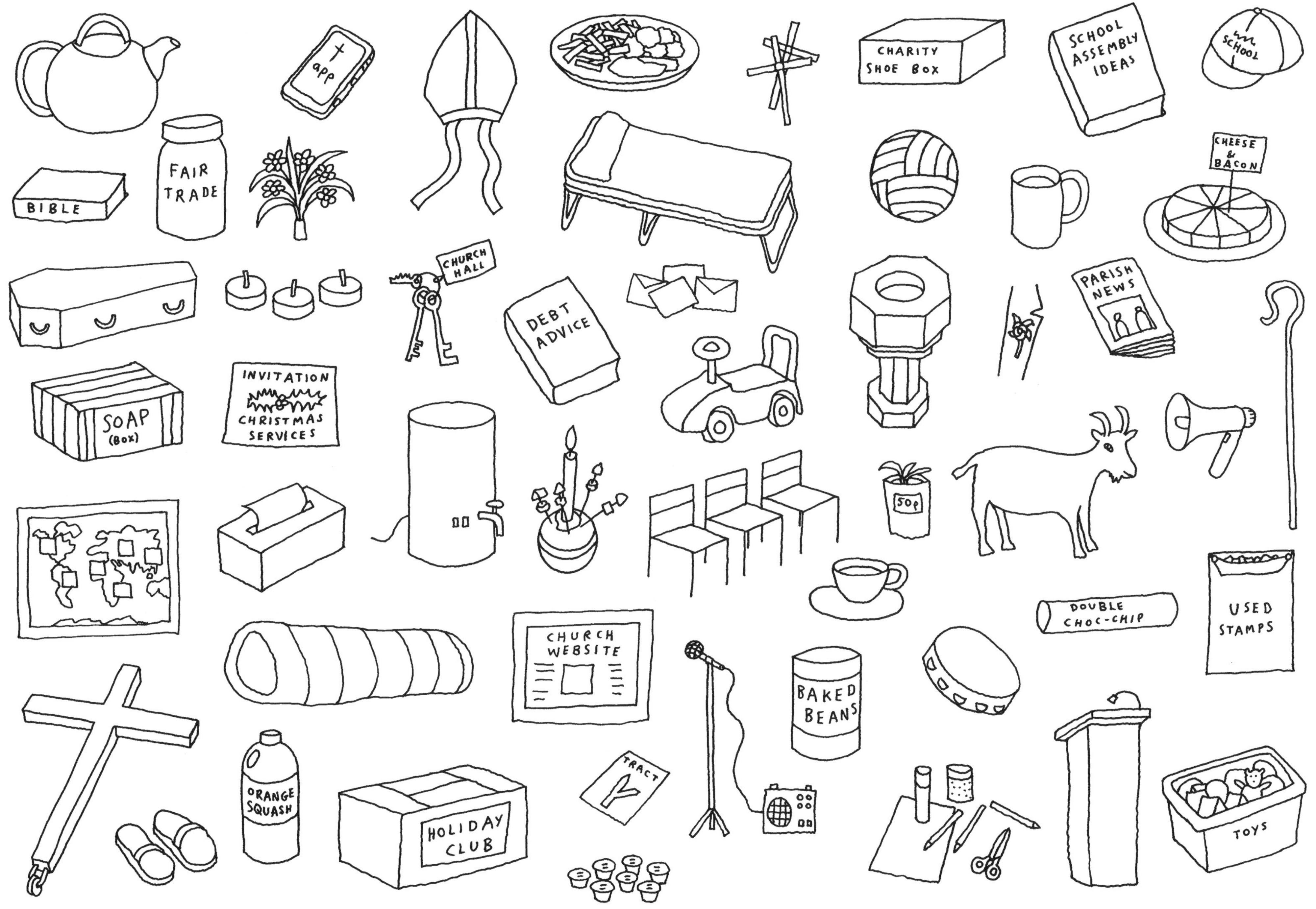
app
CHARITY SHOE BOX
SCHOOL ASSEMBLY IDEAS
SCHOOL
BIBLE
FAIR TRADE
CHEESE & BACON
CHURCH HALL
DEBT ADVICE
PARISH NEWS
INVITATION
CHRISTMAS SERVICES
SOAP (BOX)
50p
DOUBLE CHOC-CHIP
USED STAMPS
CHURCH WEBSITE
BAKED BEANS
TRACT
ORANGE SQUASH
HOLIDAY CLUB
TOYS

ARRANGING THE FLOWERS

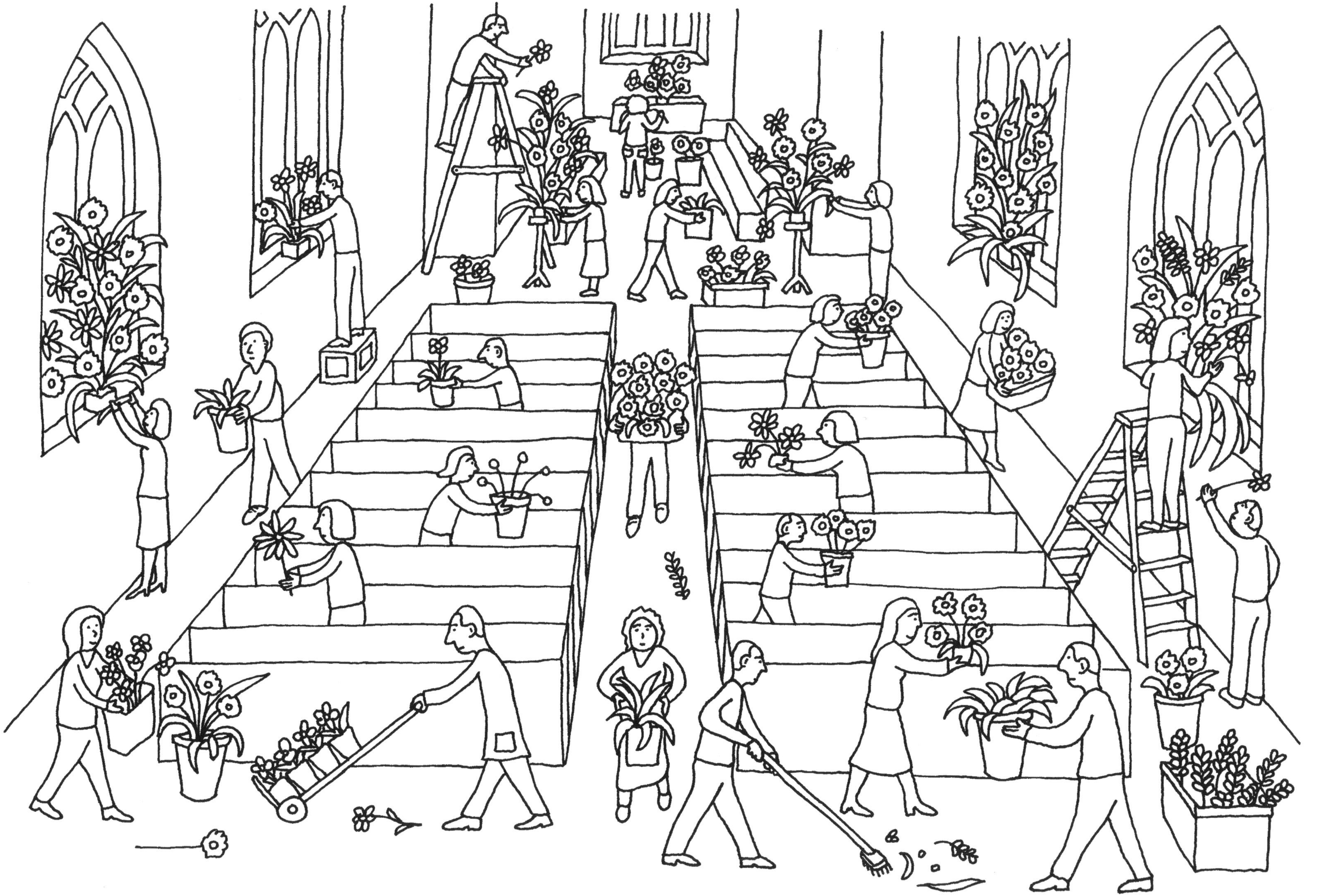

BISHOPS' LUNCHTIME

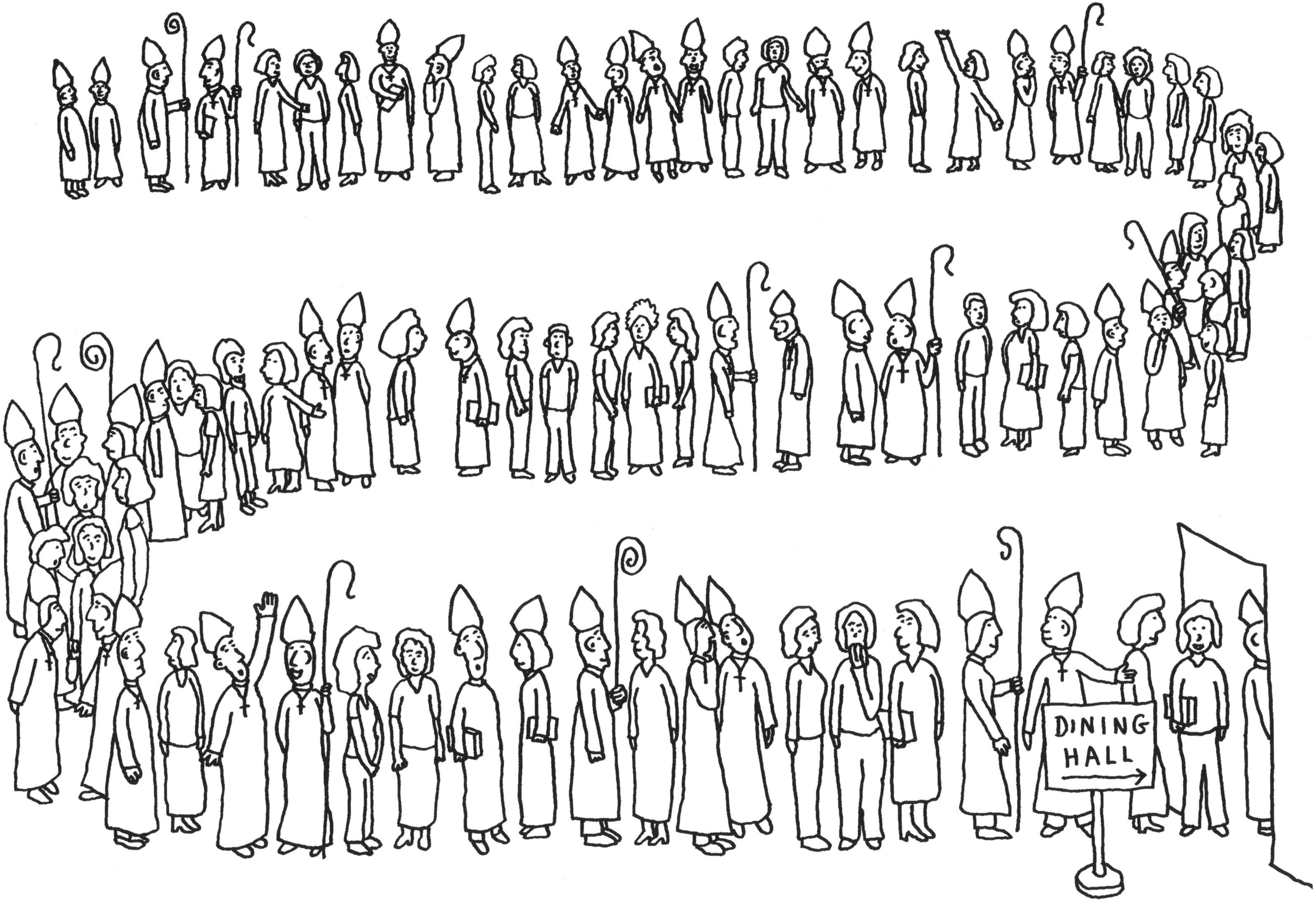
DINING HALL

THE BRING AND SHARE LUNCH

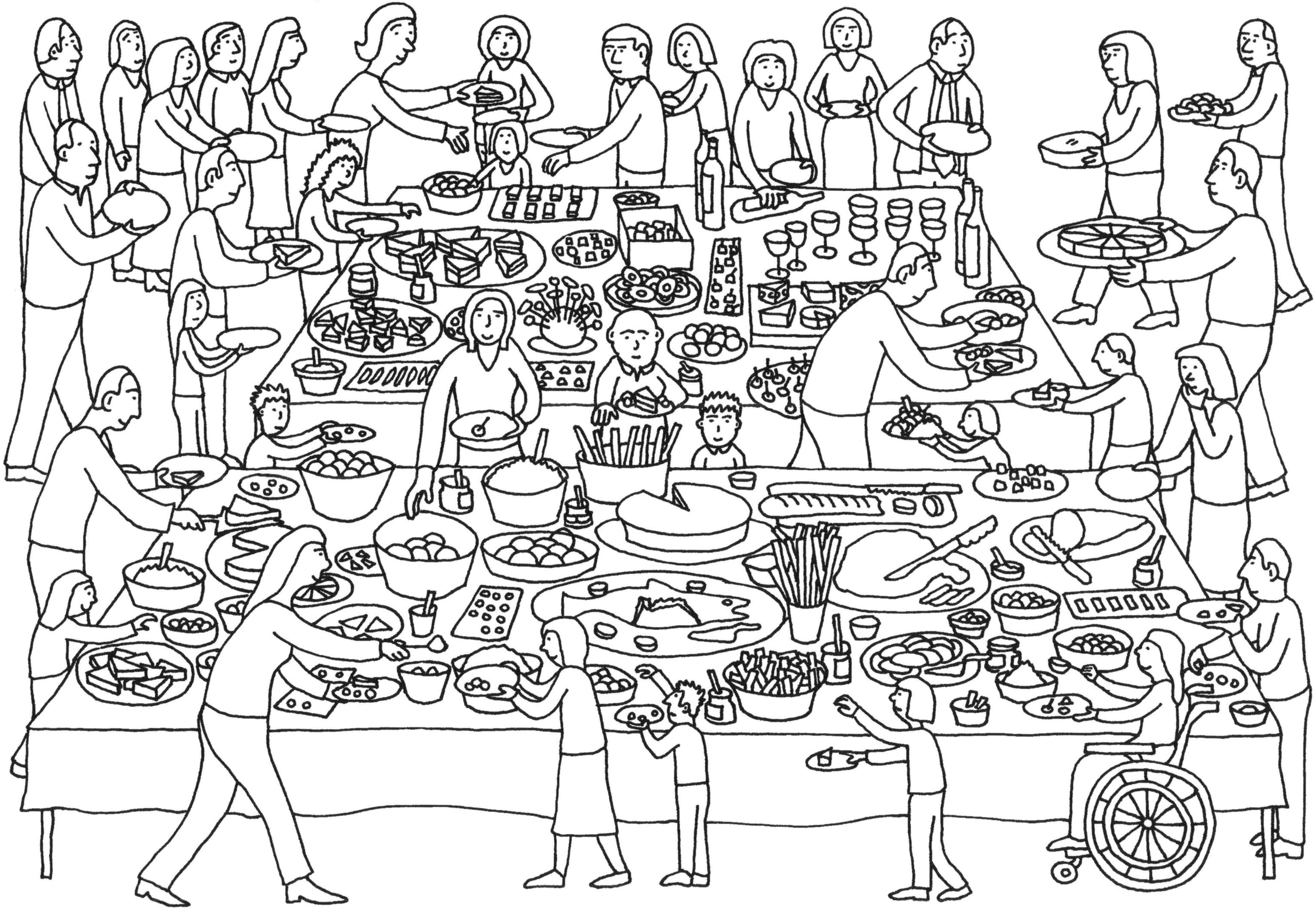

THE CATHEDRAL SHOP

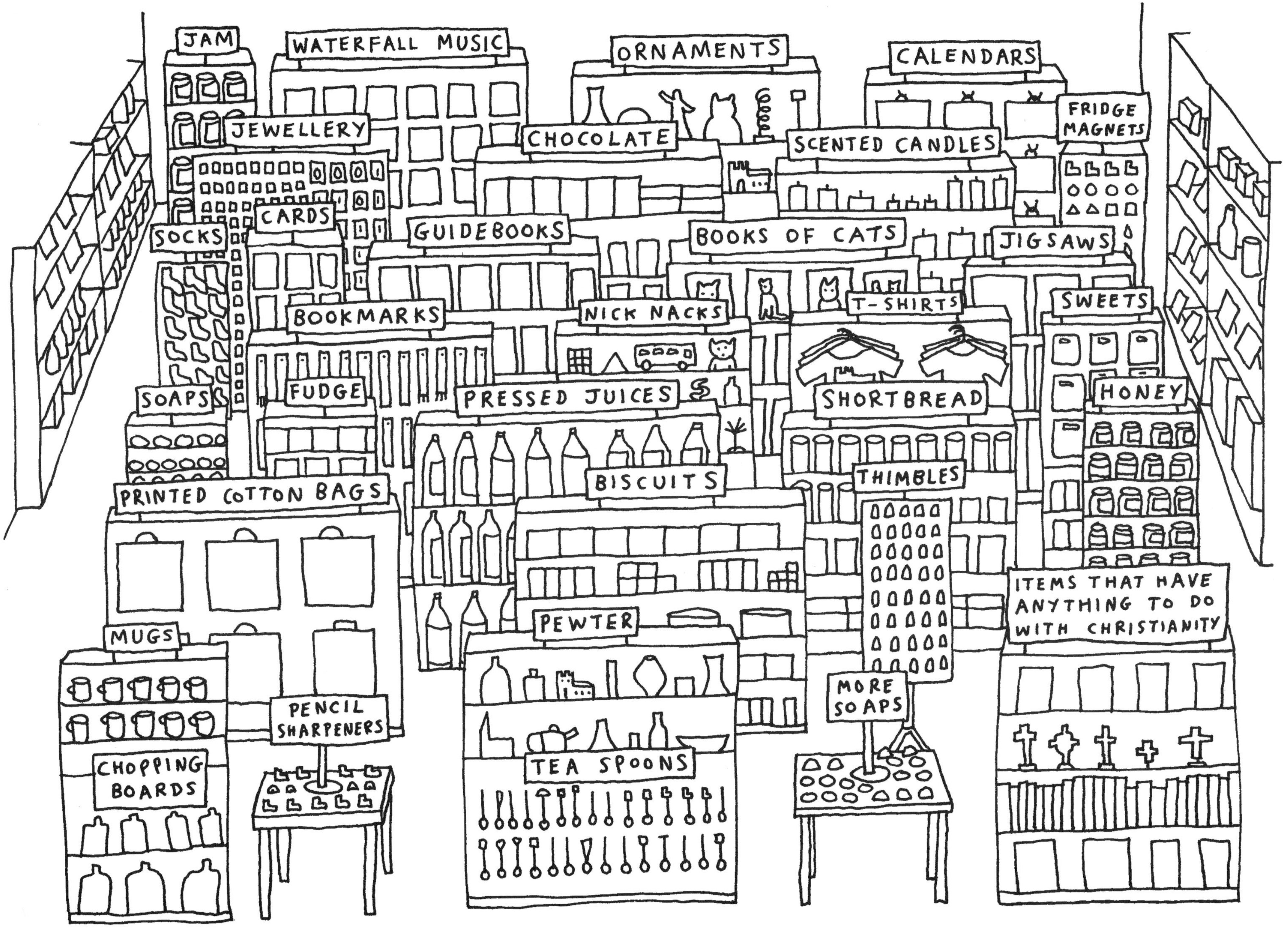

JAM
WATERFALL MUSIC
ORNAMENTS
CALENDARS
FRIDGE MAGNETS
JEWELLERY
CHOCOLATE
SCENTED CANDLES
CARDS
SOCKS
GUIDEBOOKS
BOOKS OF CATS
JIGSAWS
BOOKMARKS
NICK NACKS
T-SHIRTS
SWEETS
SOAPS
FUDGE
PRESSED JUICES
SHORTBREAD
HONEY
PRINTED COTTON BAGS
BISCUITS
THIMBLES
ITEMS THAT HAVE ANYTHING TO DO WITH CHRISTIANITY
MUGS
PEWTER
PENCIL SHARPENERS
MORE SOAPS
CHOPPING BOARDS
TEA SPOONS

THE CHOIR

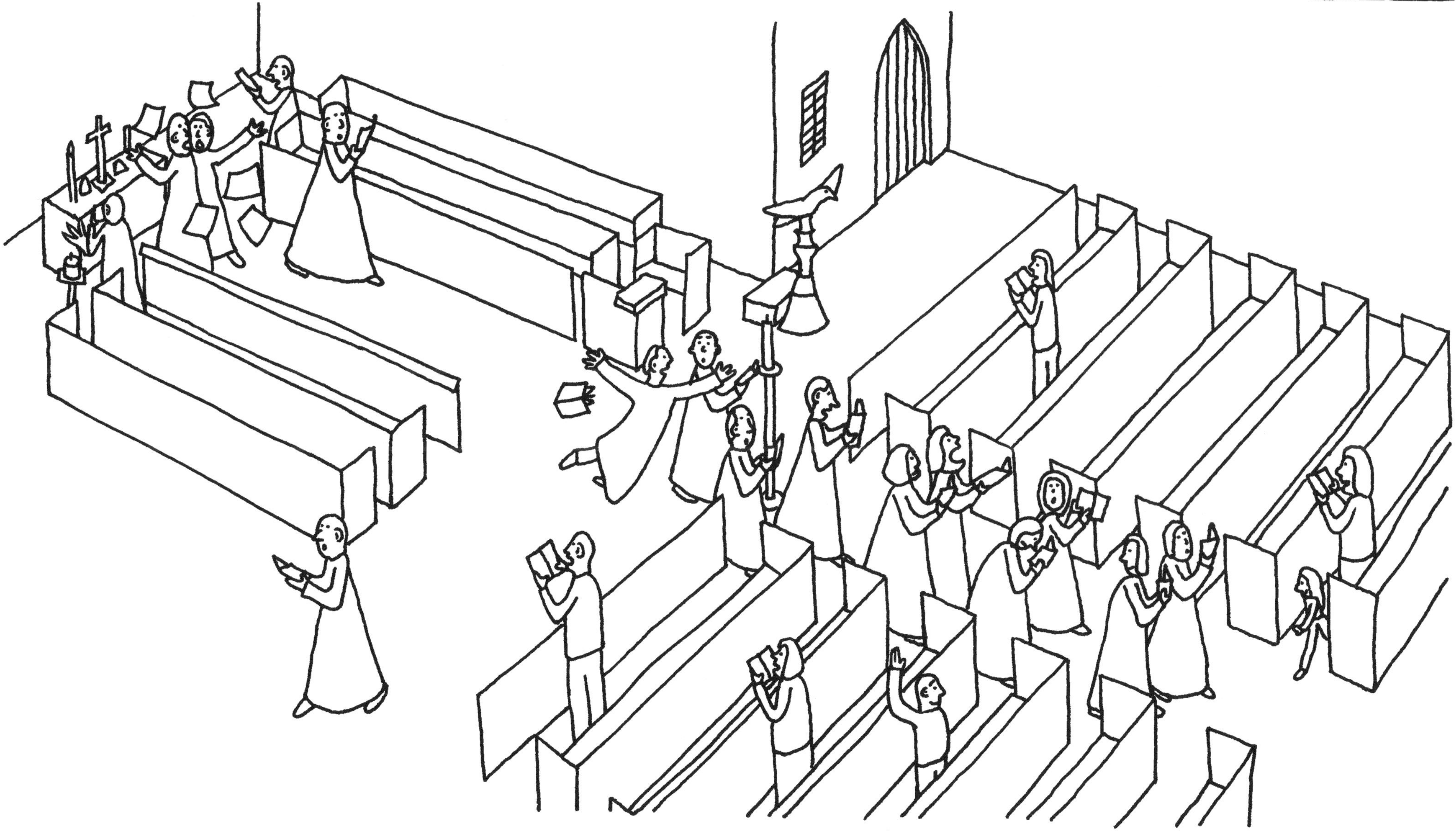

THE CHRISTIAN CONFERENCE

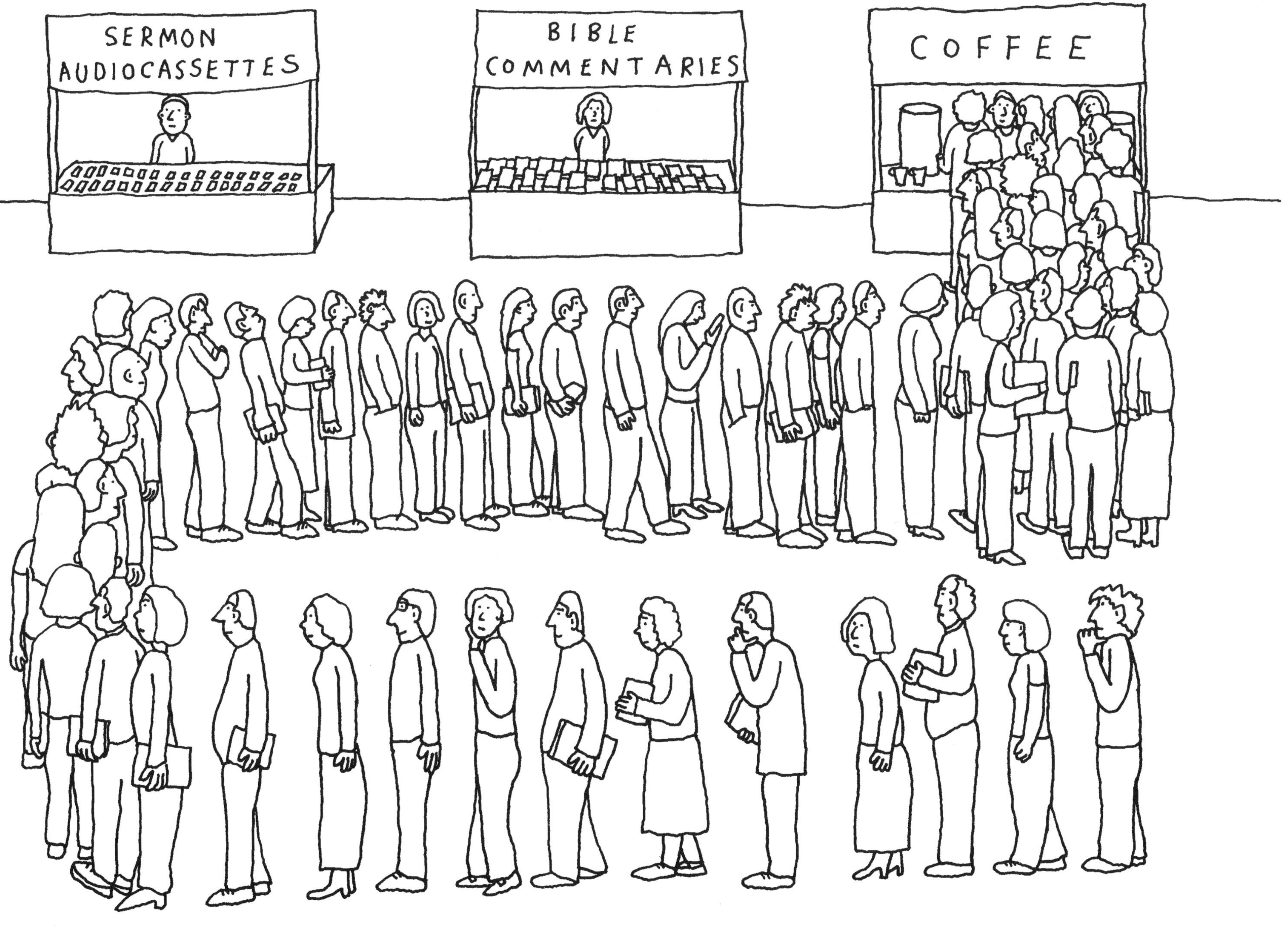
SERMON AUDIOCASSETTES
BIBLE COMMENTARIES
COFFEE

THE CHURCH IN THE CITY

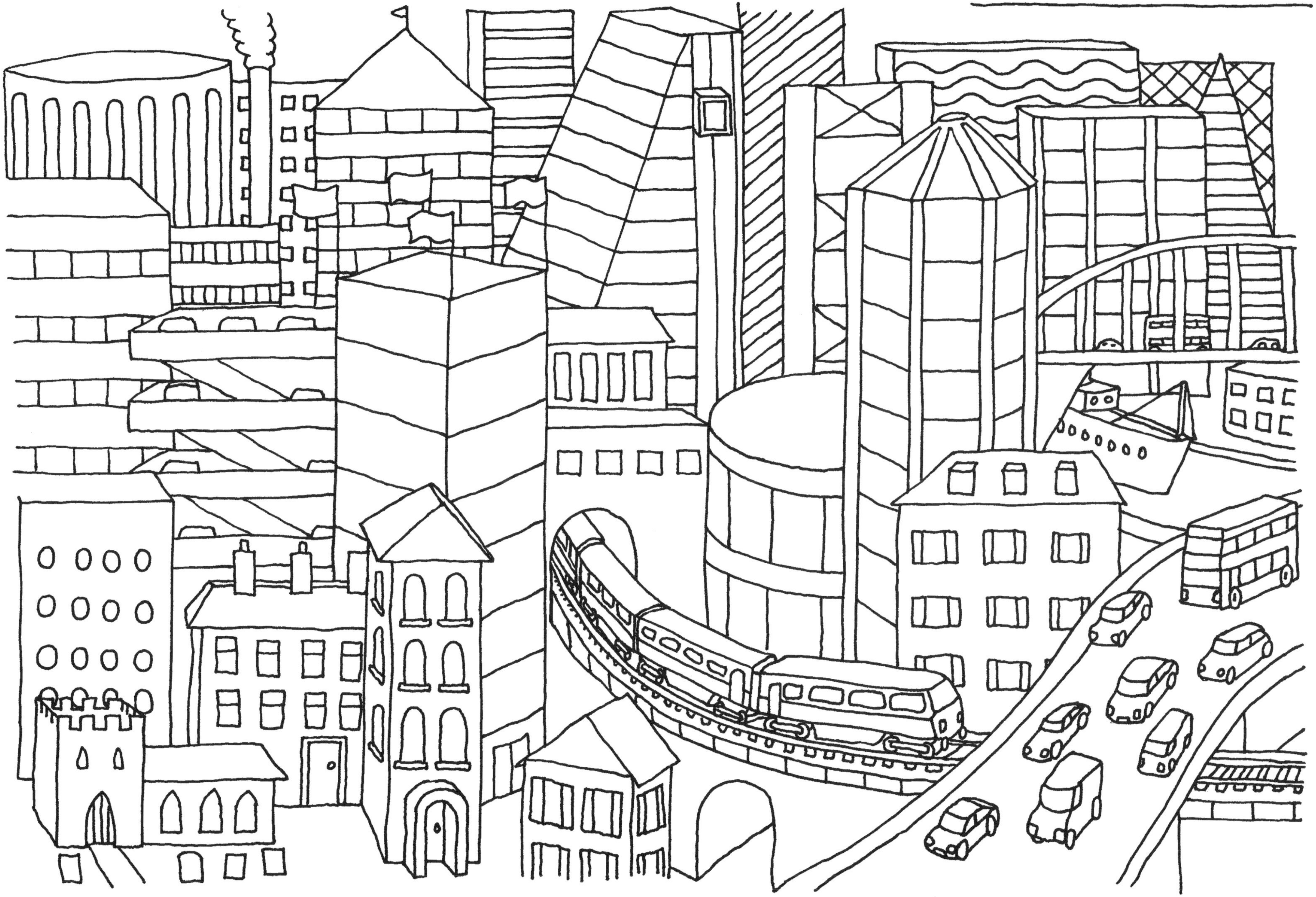

THE CHURCH KITCHEN

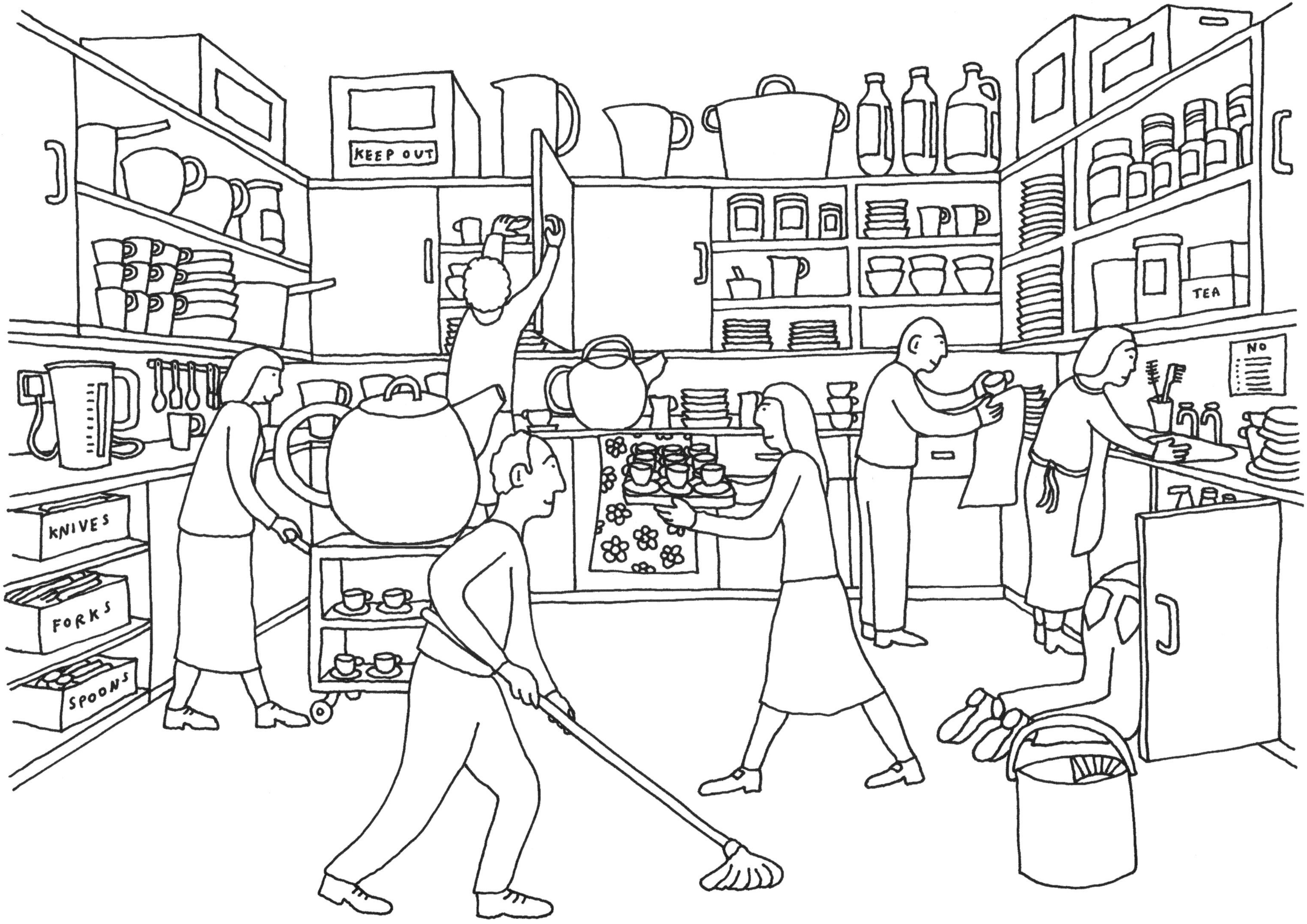
KEEP OUT
TEA
NO
KNIVES
FORKS
SPOONS

THE CLEANING CUPBOARD

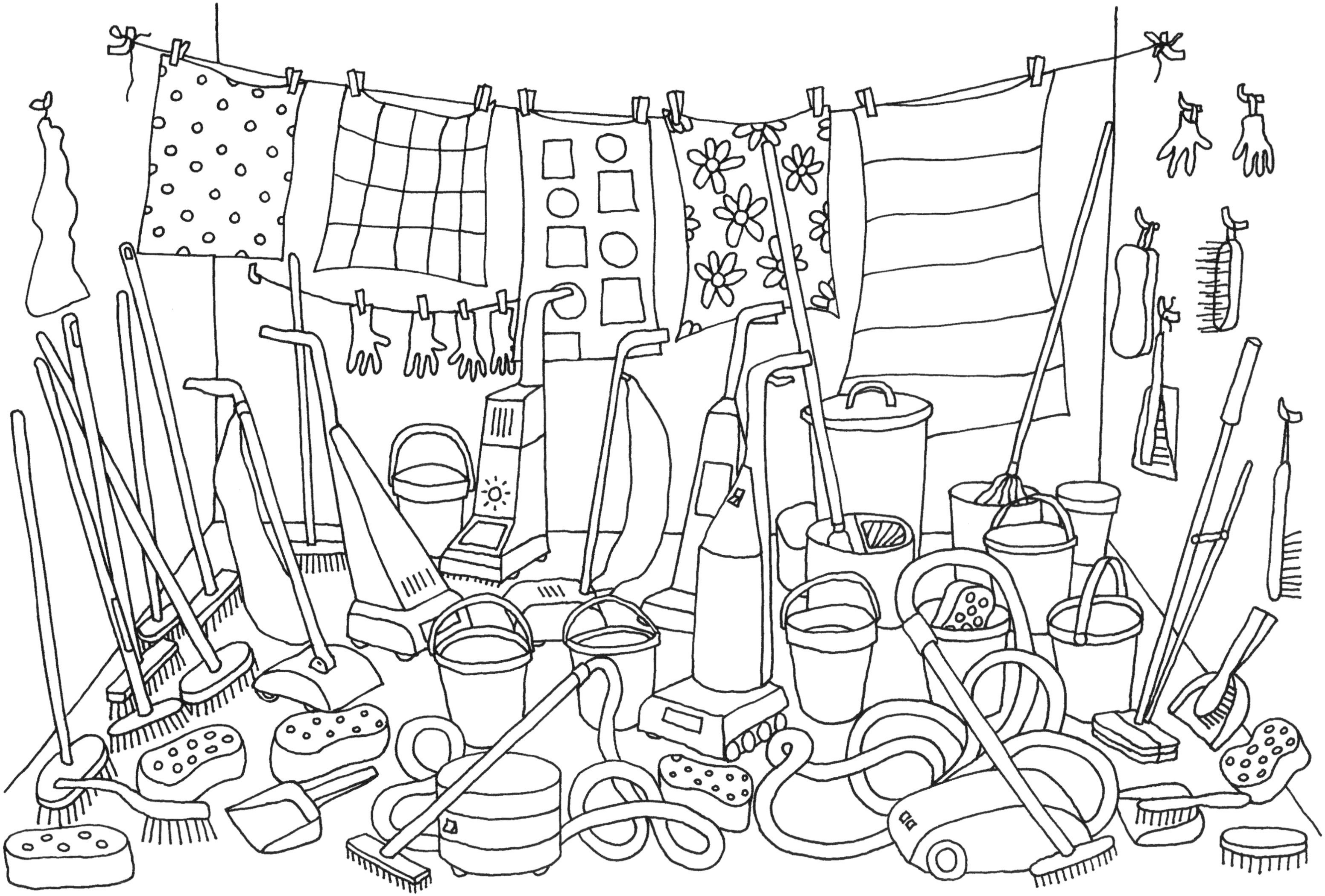

THE CLERGY CONFERENCE

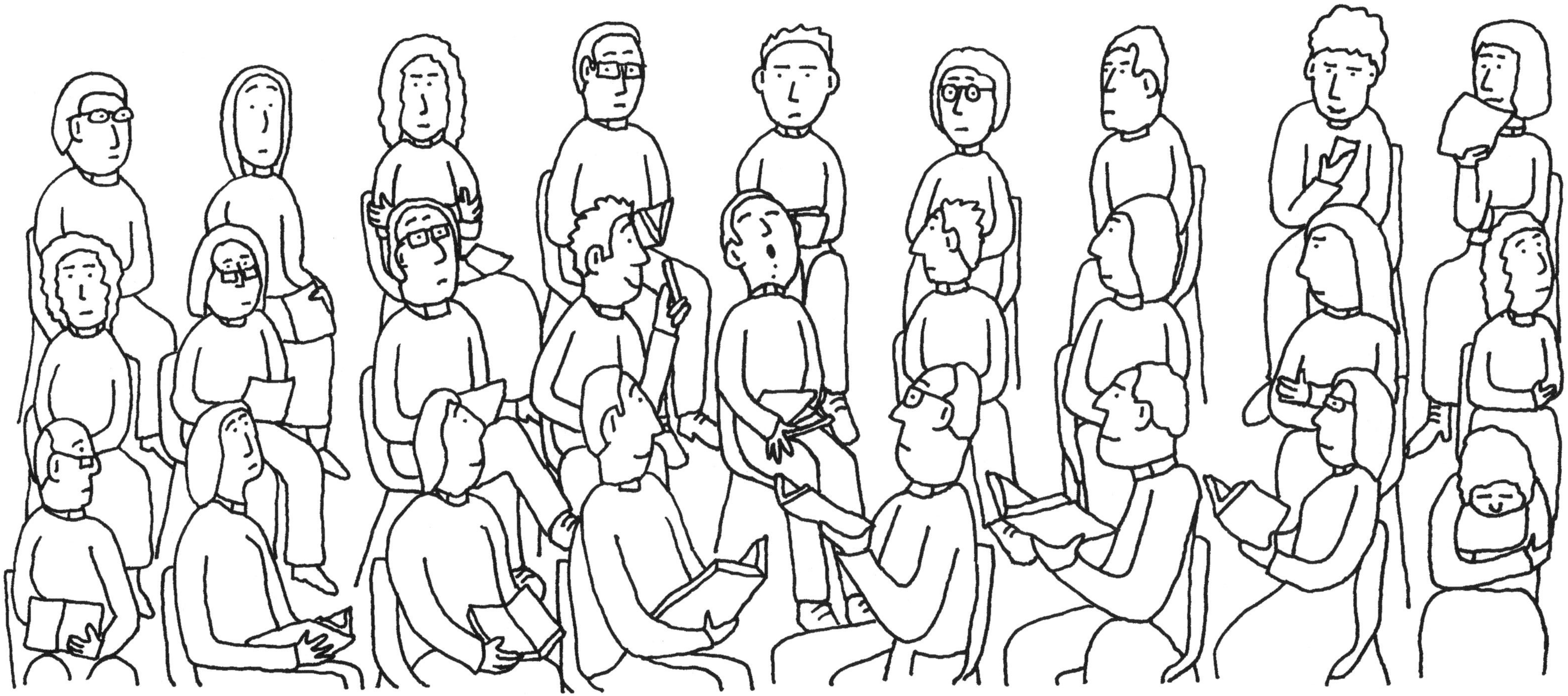

THE CLERICAL OUTFITTERS

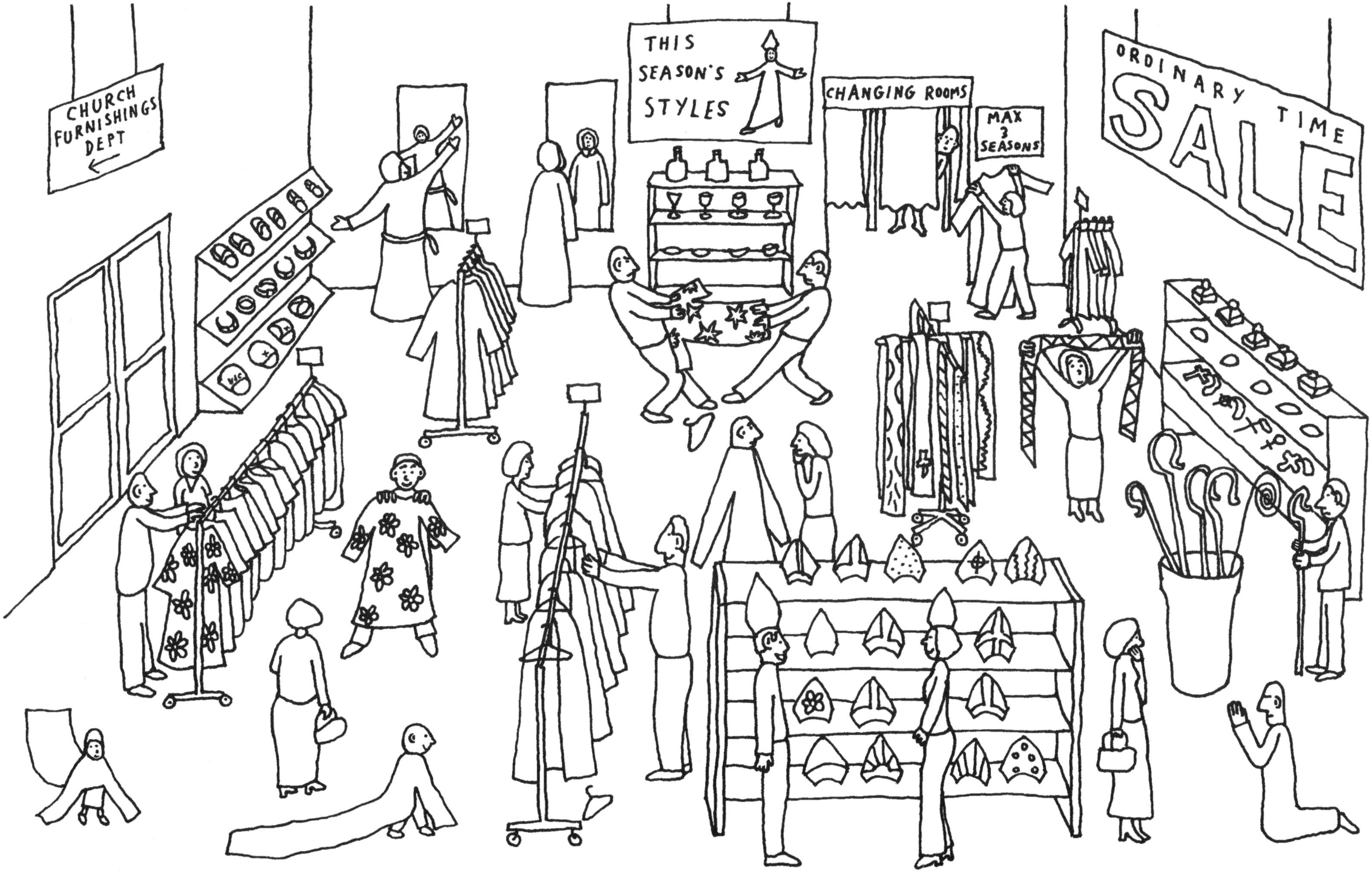
CHURCH FURNISHINGS DEPT ←
THIS SEASON'S STYLES
CHANGING ROOMS
MAX 3 SEASONS
ORDINARY TIME SALE

COFFEE TIME

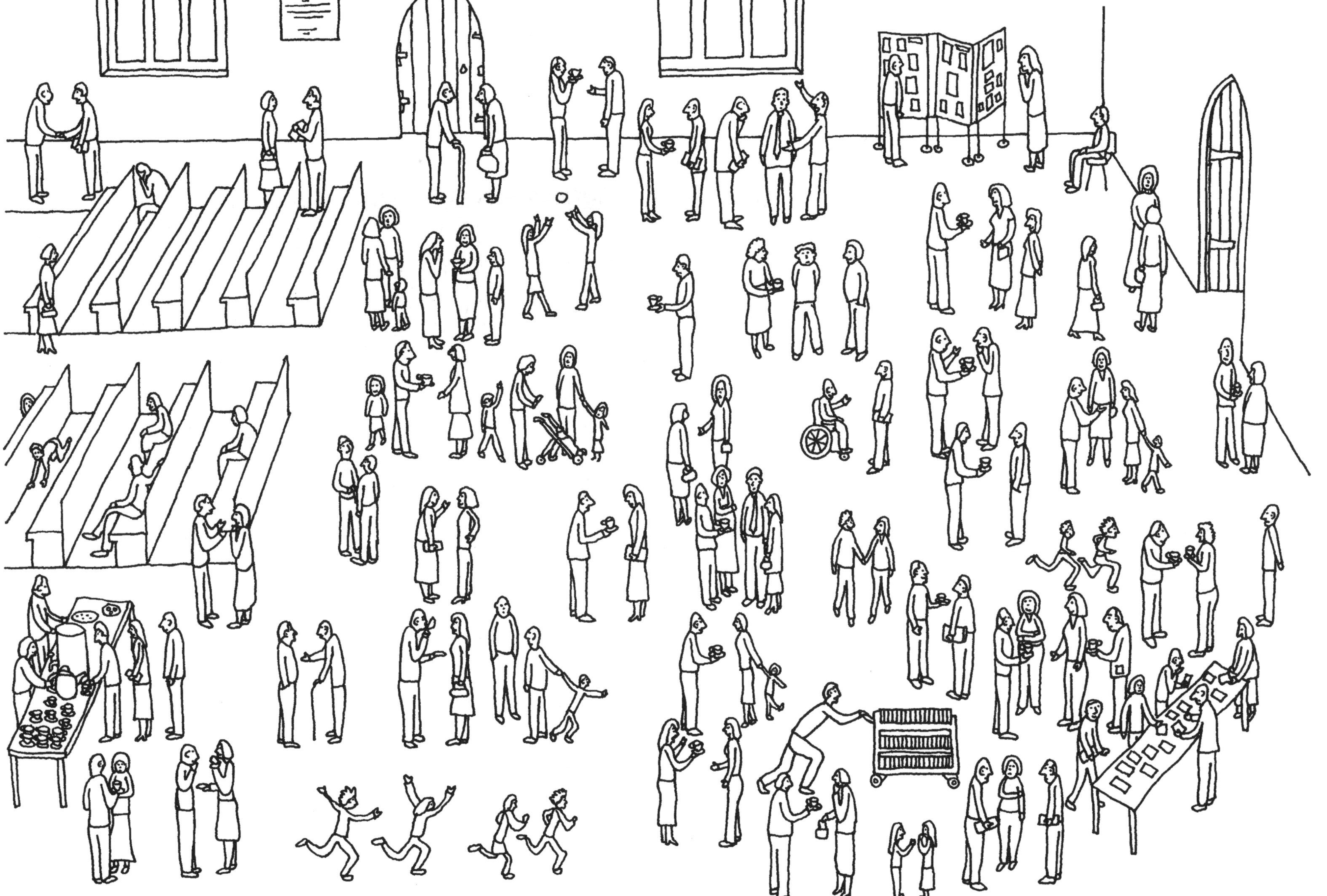

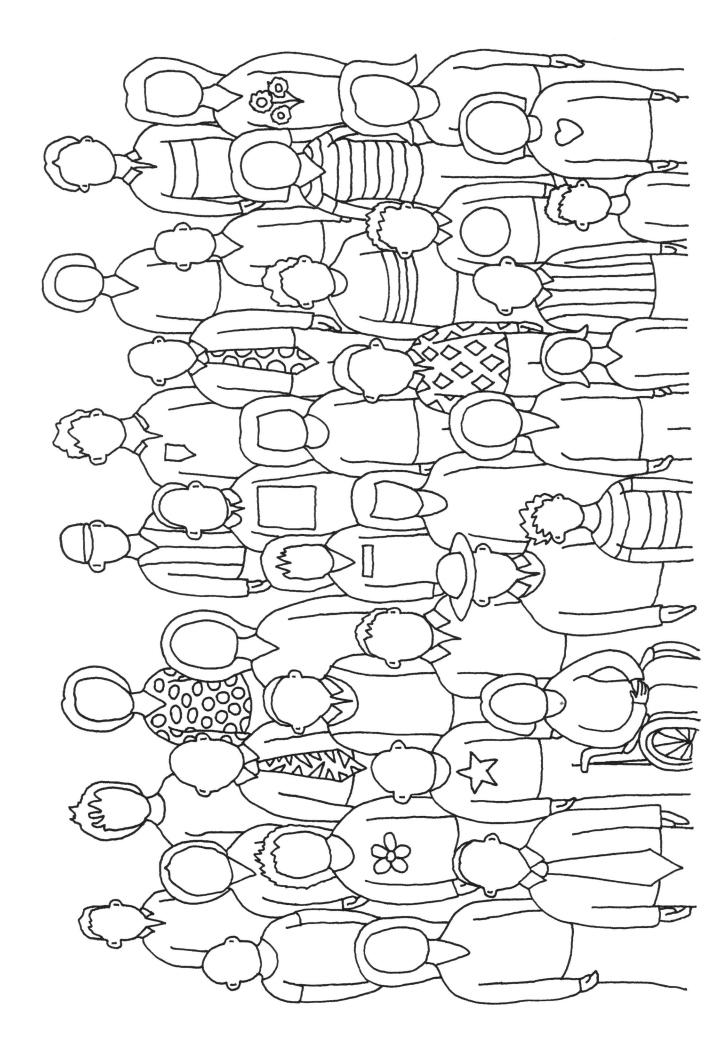

FESTIVAL SCENES

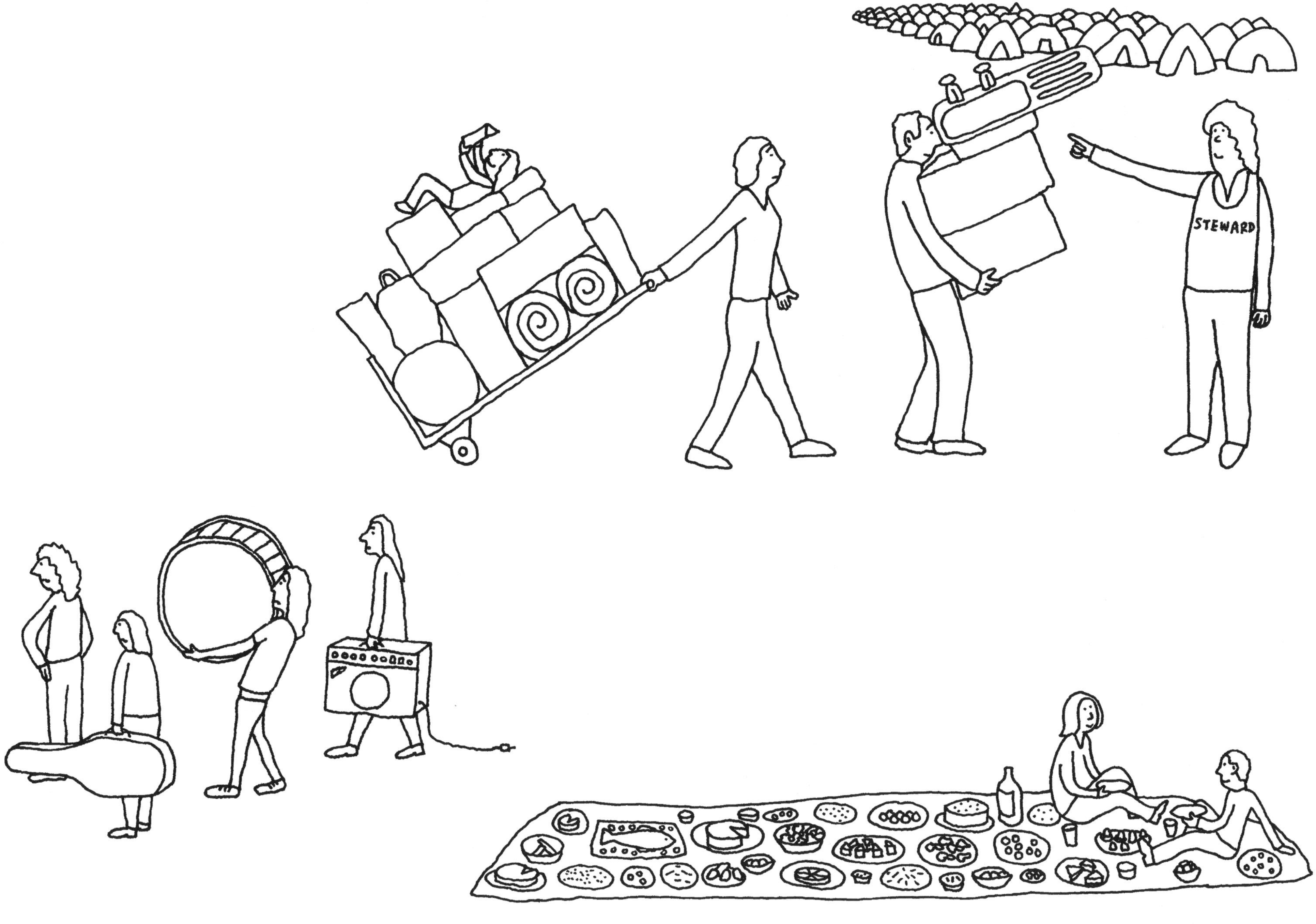
STEWARD

THE FETE

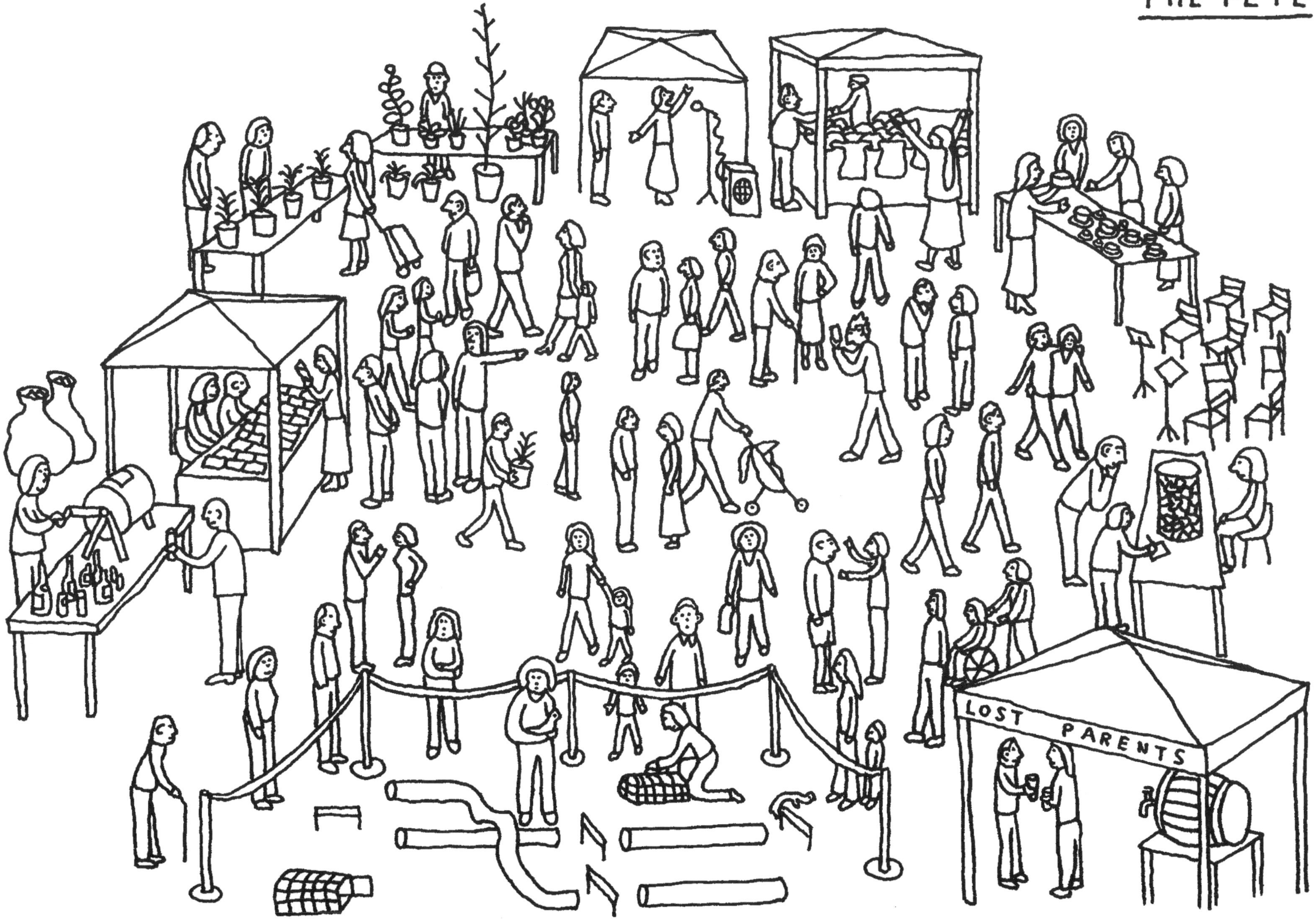

LOST PARENTS

THE VERGER'S OFFICE

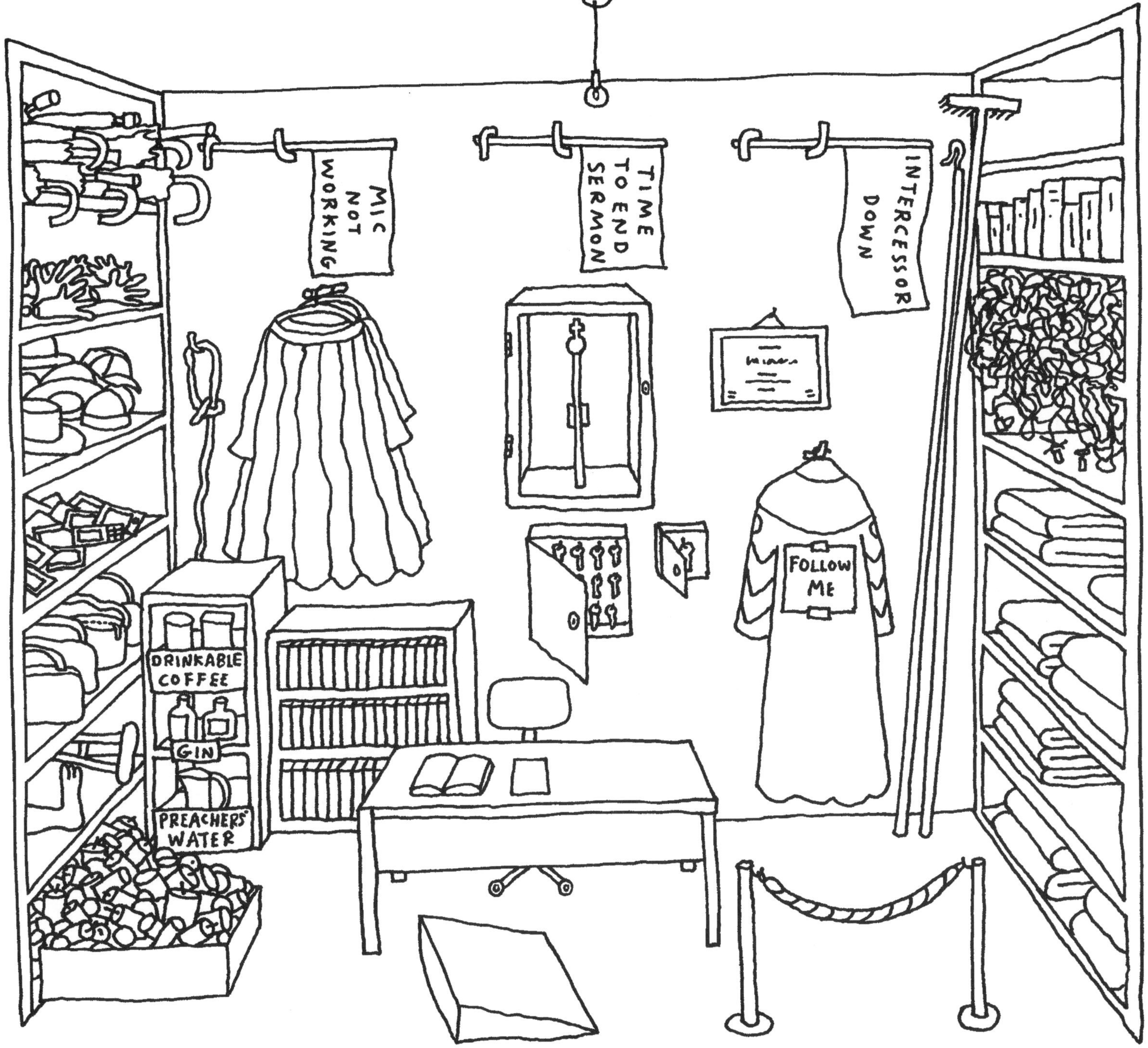
MIC NOT WORKING
TIME TO END SERMON
INTERCESSOR DOWN
FOLLOW ME
DRINKABLE COFFEE
GIN
PREACHERS' WATER

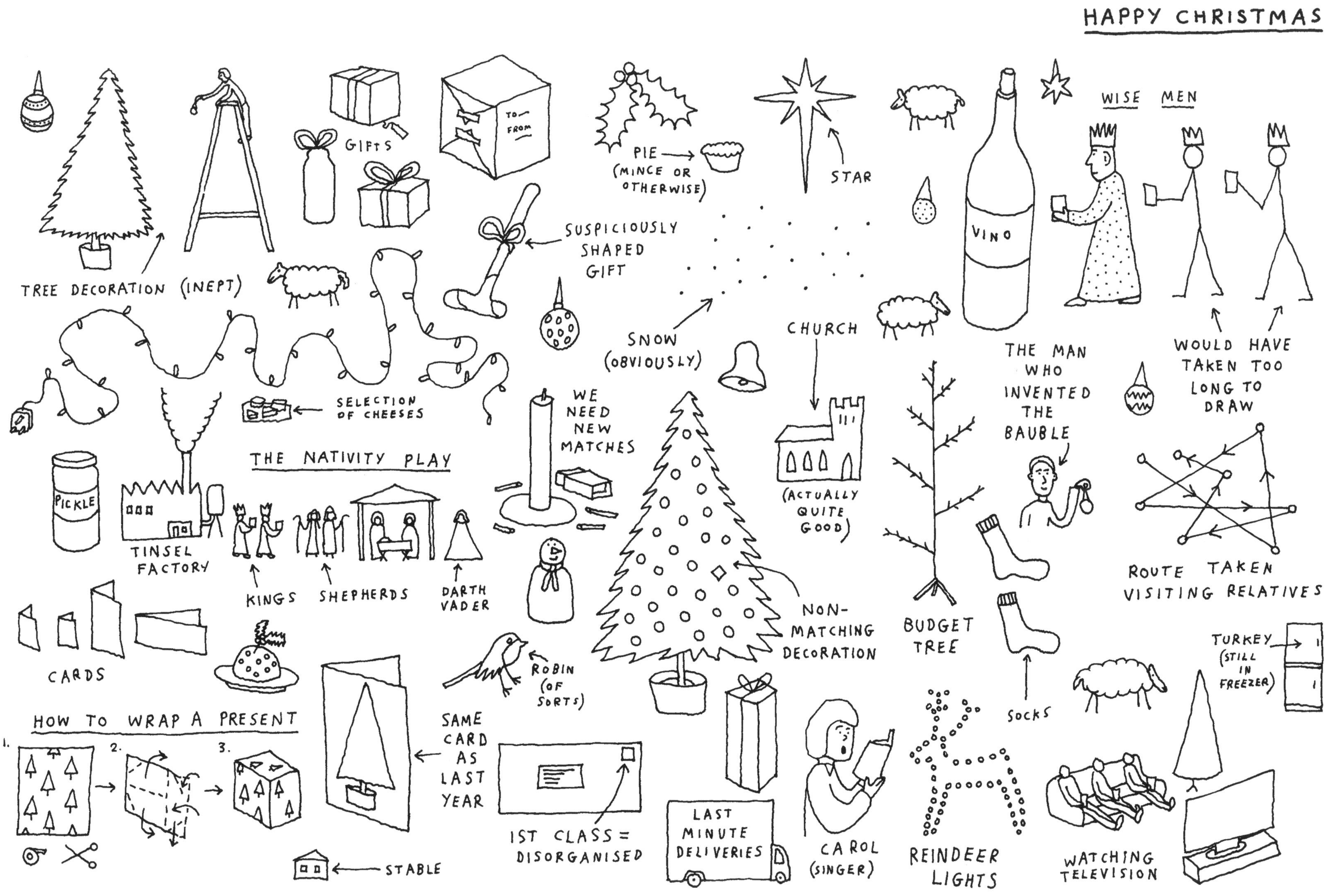
HAPPY CHRISTMAS
TREE DECORATION (INEPT)
GIFTS
TO—
FROM
PIE
(MINCE OR OTHERWISE)
STAR
SUSPICIOUSLY SHAPED GIFT
SNOW (OBVIOUSLY)
VINO
WISE MEN
WOULD HAVE TAKEN TOO LONG TO DRAW
CHURCH
(ACTUALLY QUITE GOOD)
THE MAN WHO INVENTED THE BAUBLE
ROUTE TAKEN VISITING RELATIVES
SELECTION OF CHEESES
WE NEED NEW MATCHES
THE NATIVITY PLAY
PICKLE
TINSEL FACTORY
KINGS
SHEPHERDS
DARTH VADER
NON-MATCHING DECORATION
BUDGET TREE
SOCKS
TURKEY (STILL IN FREEZER)
CARDS
ROBIN (OF SORTS)
HOW TO WRAP A PRESENT
1.
2.
3.
SAME CARD AS LAST YEAR
1ST CLASS = DISORGANISED
LAST MINUTE DELIVERIES
CAROL (SINGER)
REINDEER LIGHTS
WATCHING TELEVISION
STABLE

THE HEART OF THE COMMUNITY

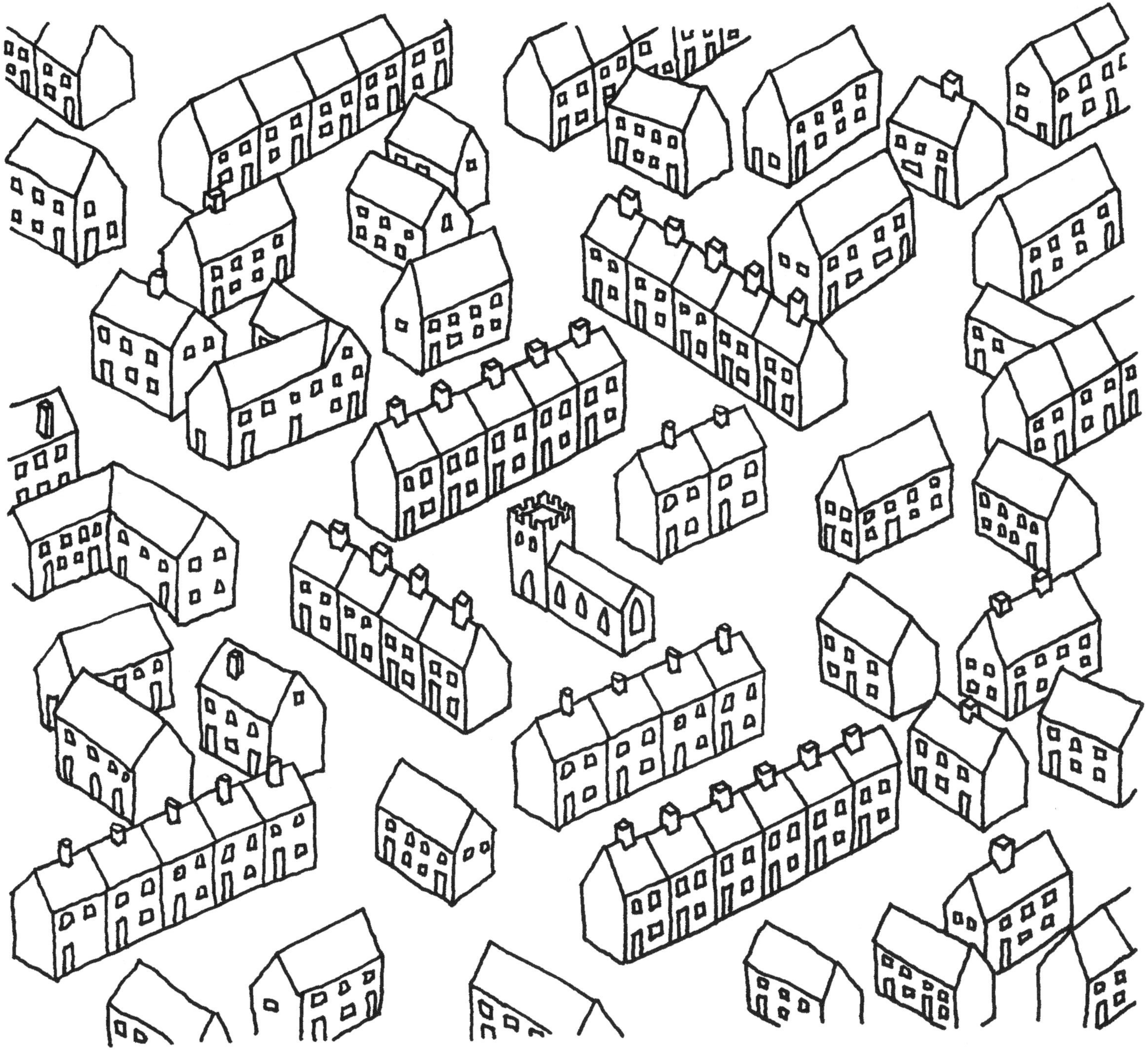

THE CHURCH HEATING SYSTEM

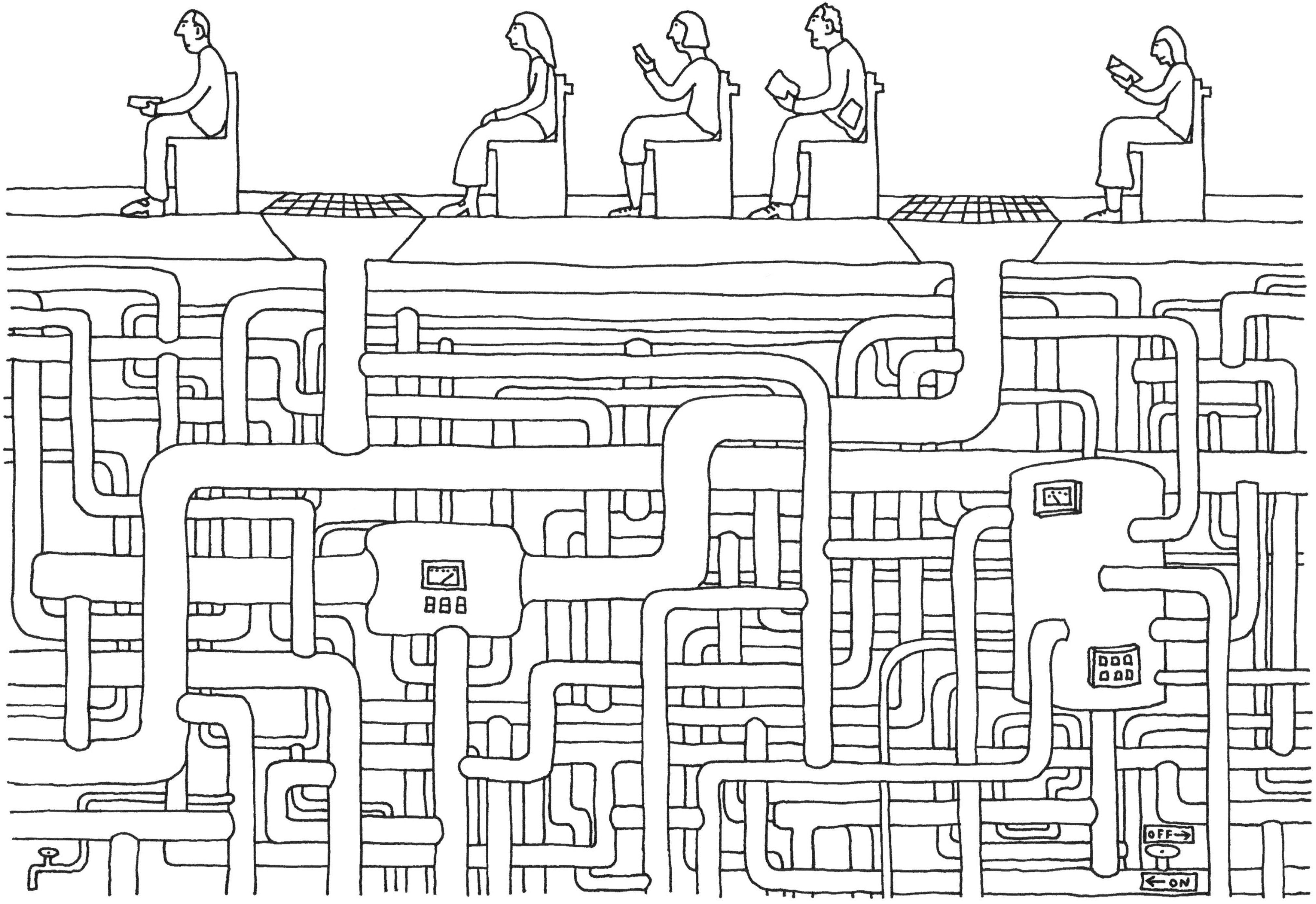
OFF→
←ON

HOW TO ESCAPE

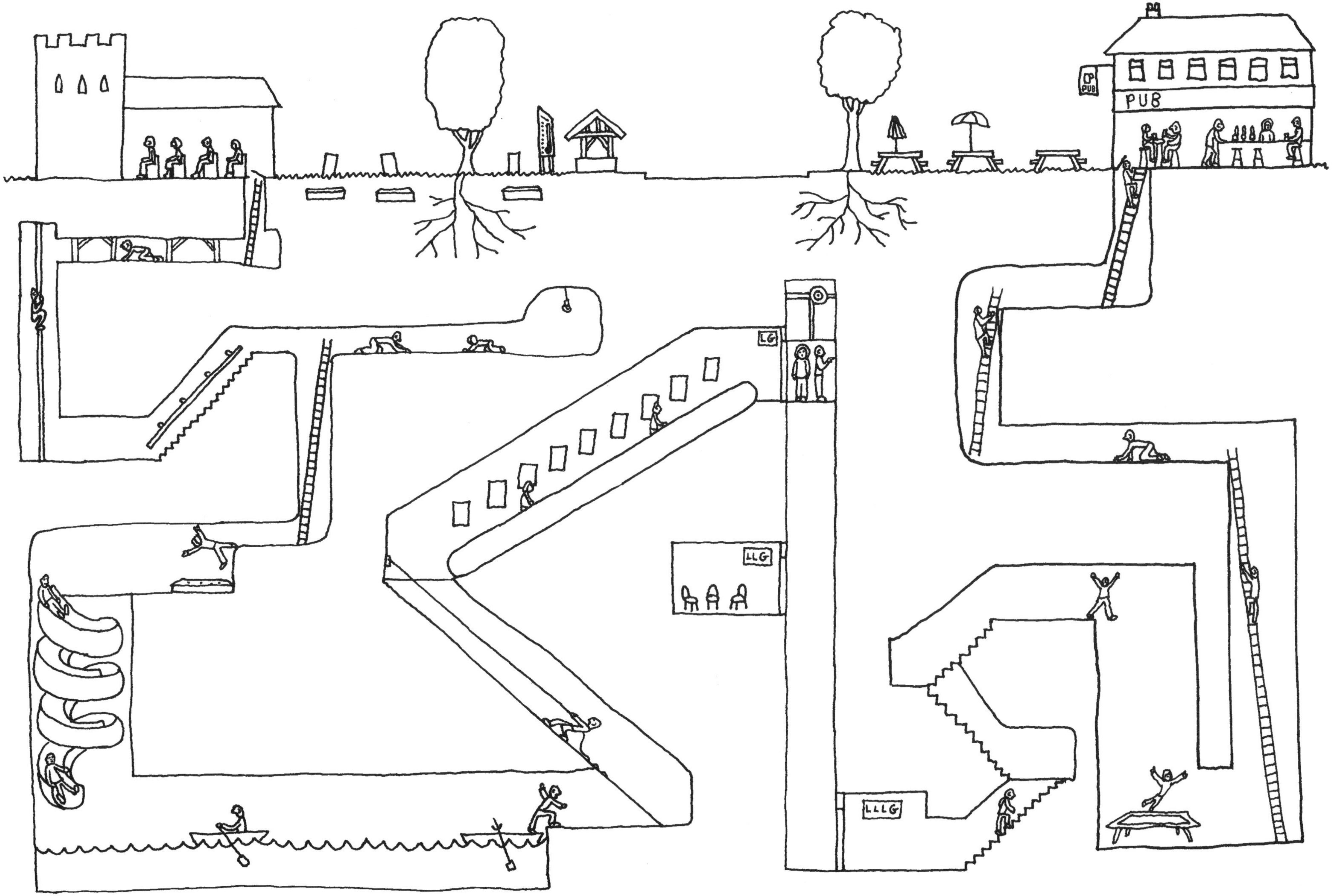
PUB
PUB
LG
LLG
LLLG

THE INTERCESSIONS

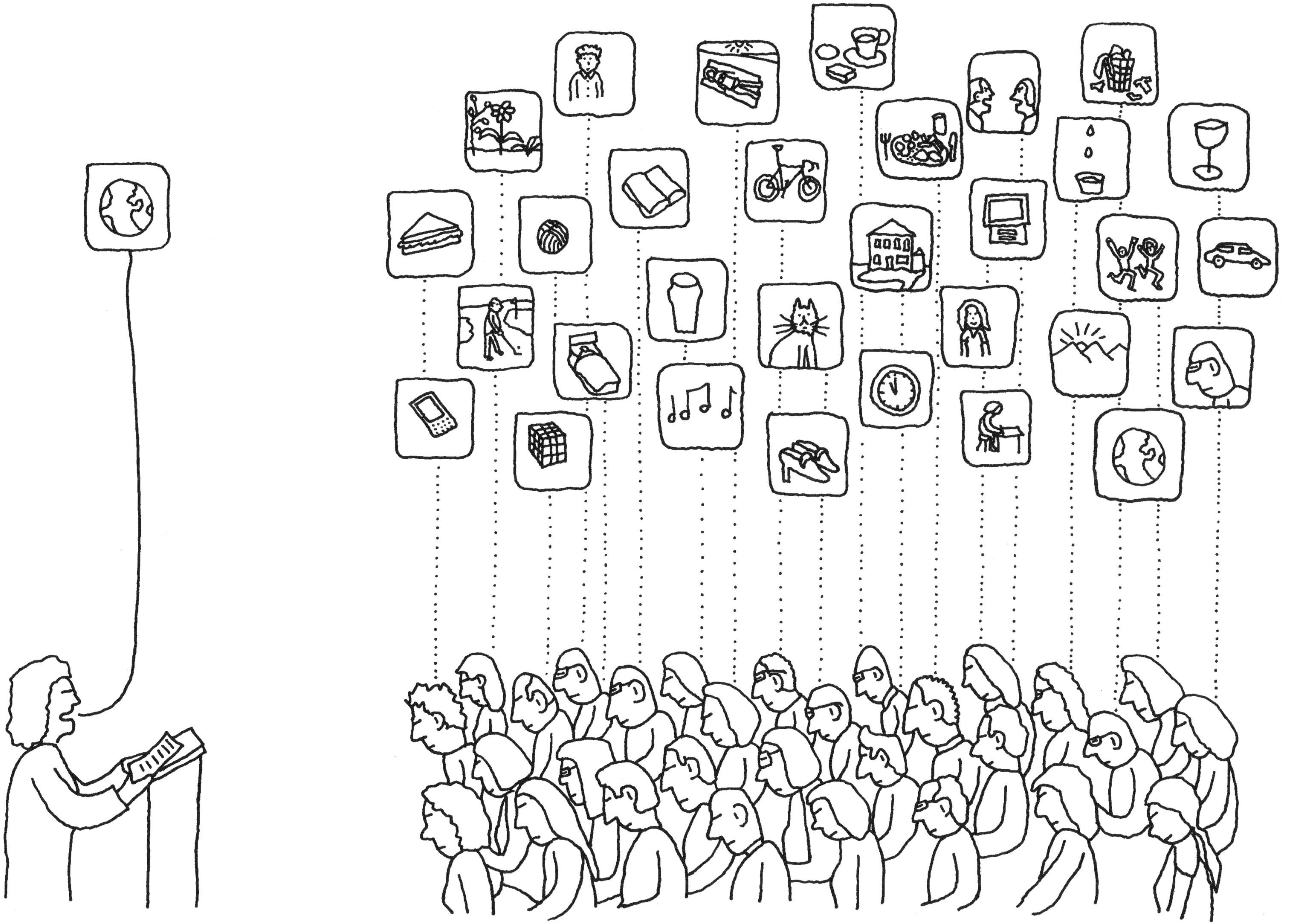

IT ALL HAPPENS HERE

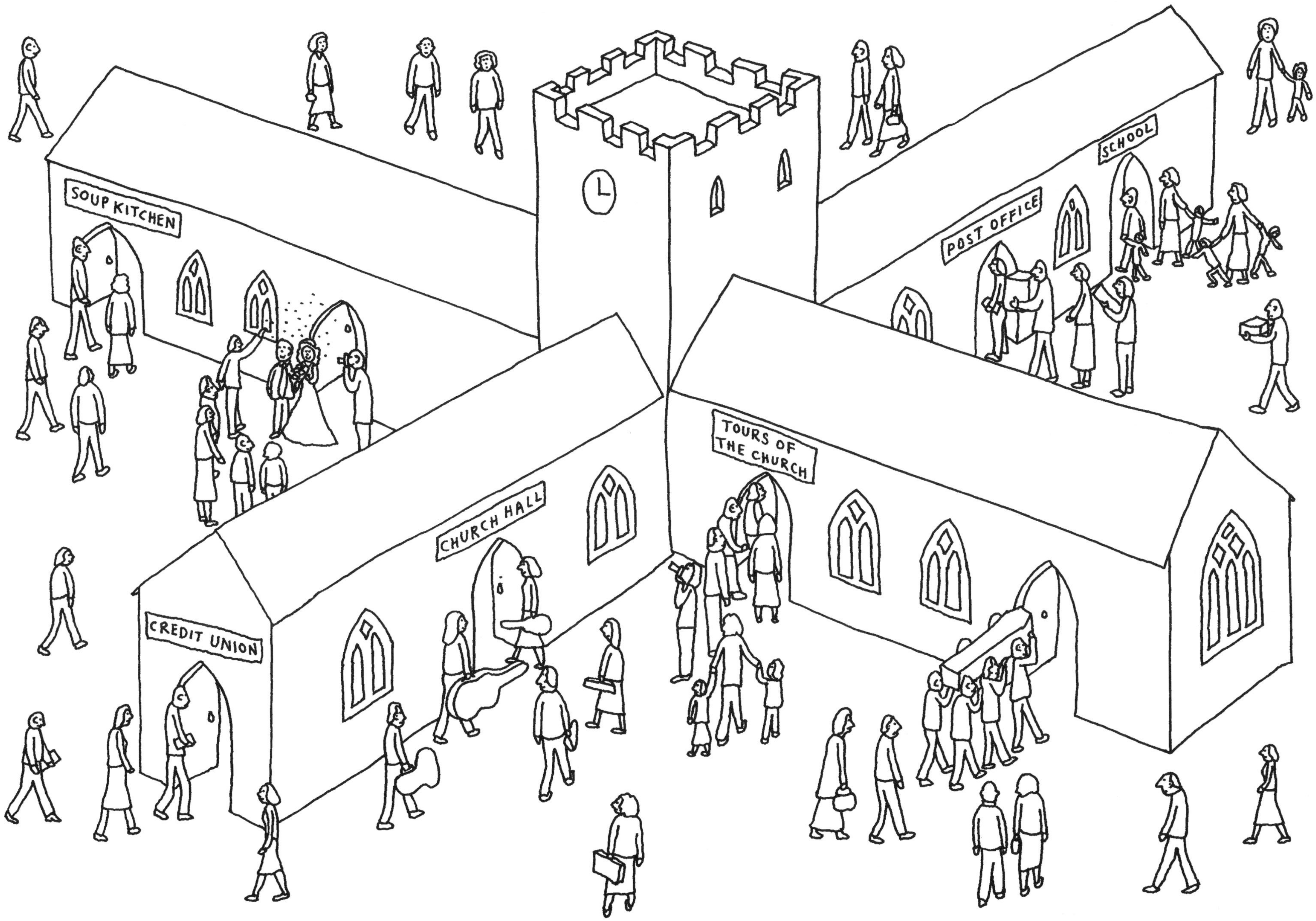
SOUP KITCHEN
SCHOOL
POST OFFICE
TOURS OF THE CHURCH
CHURCH HALL
CREDIT UNION

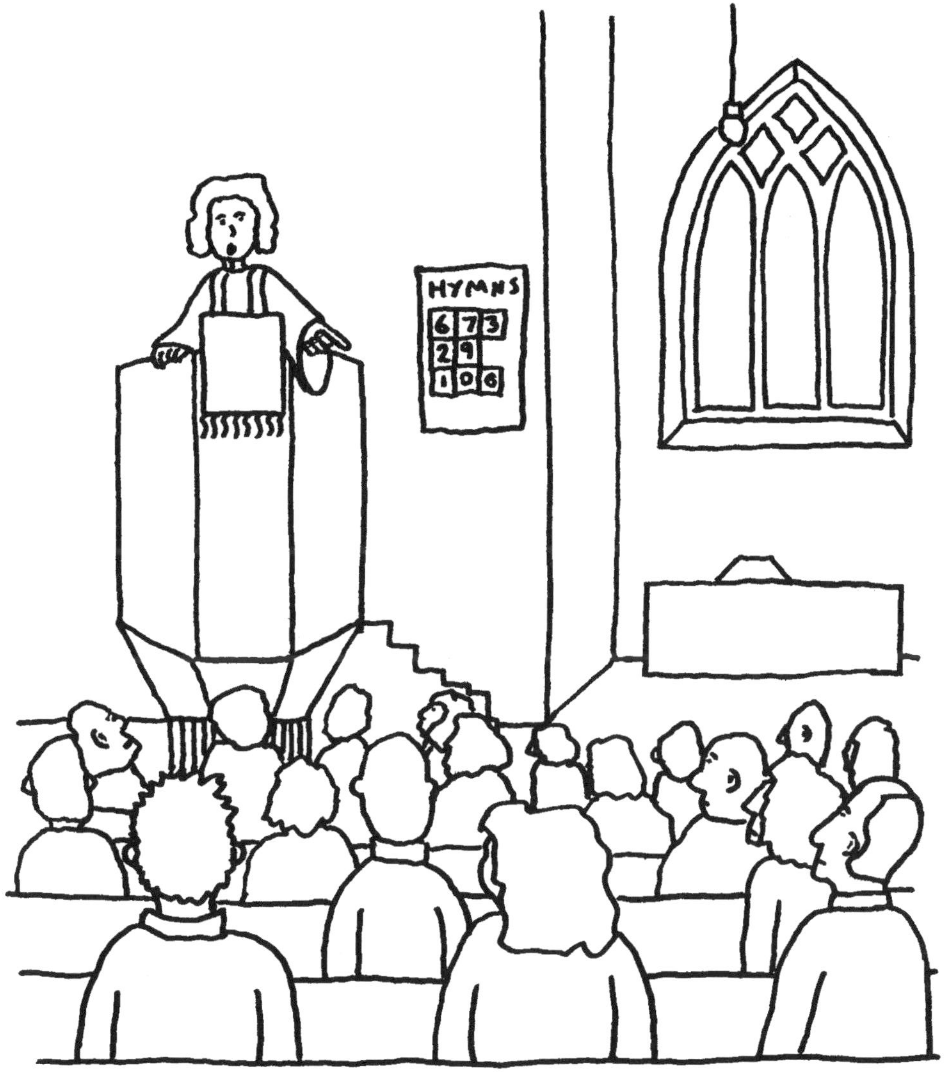
HYMNS
6 7 3
2 9
1 0 6

PRIEST IN CHARGE

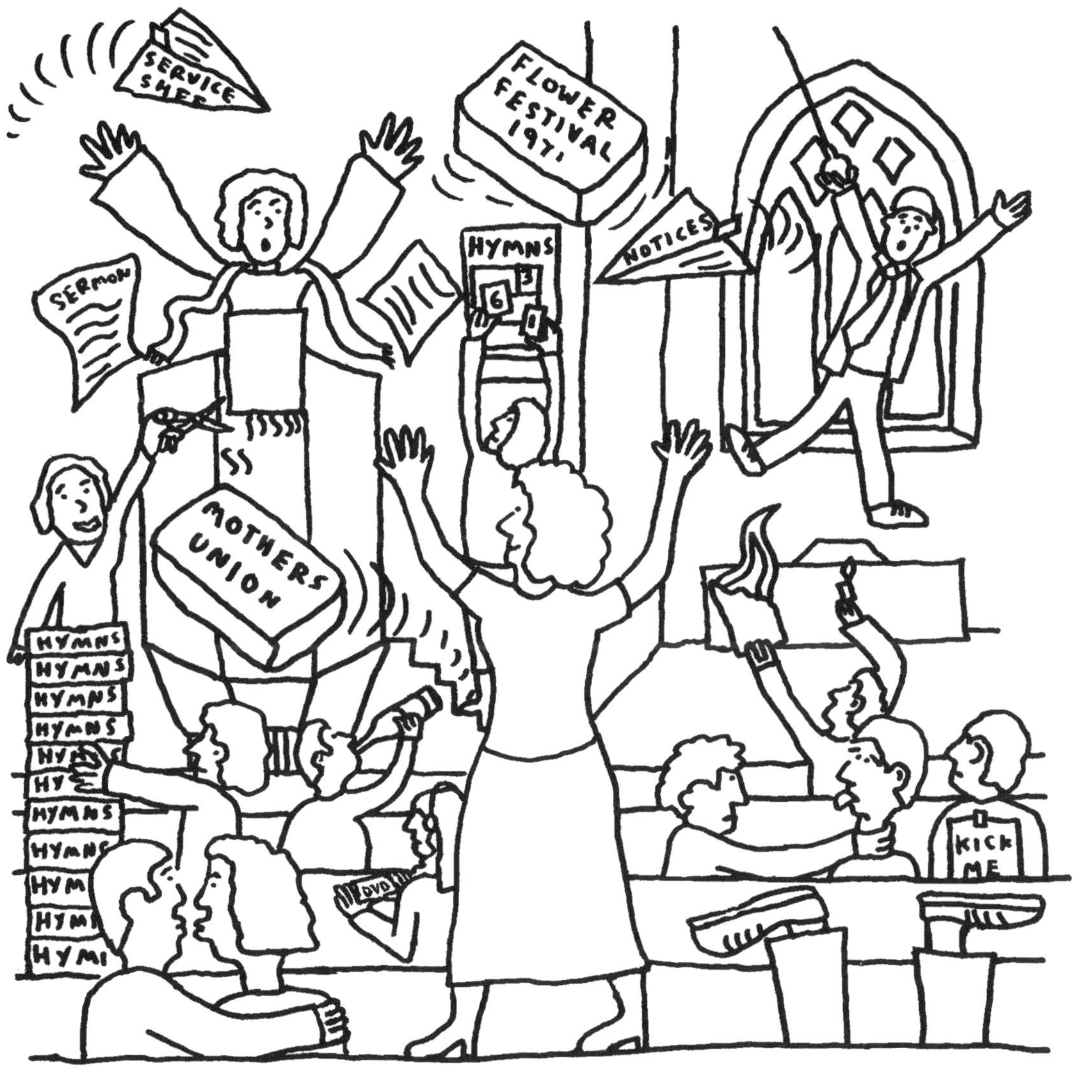
SERVICE SHEE
FLOWER FESTIVAL 1971
NOTICES
SERMON
HYMNS
MOTHERS UNION
HYMNS
DVD
KICK ME

PRIEST NOT IN CHARGE

THE CHURCH LIBRARY

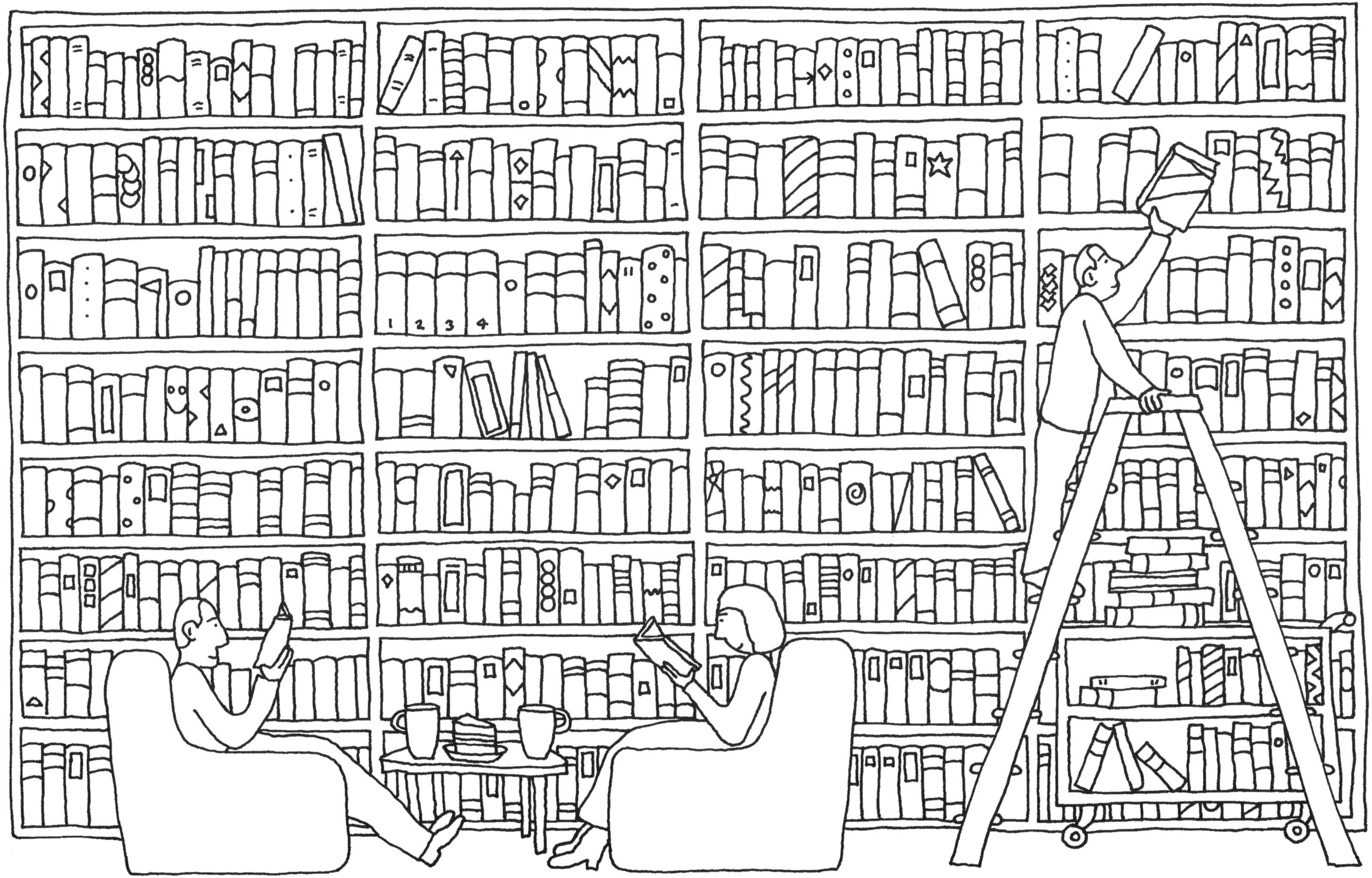
1 2 3 4

THE NATIVITY PLAY

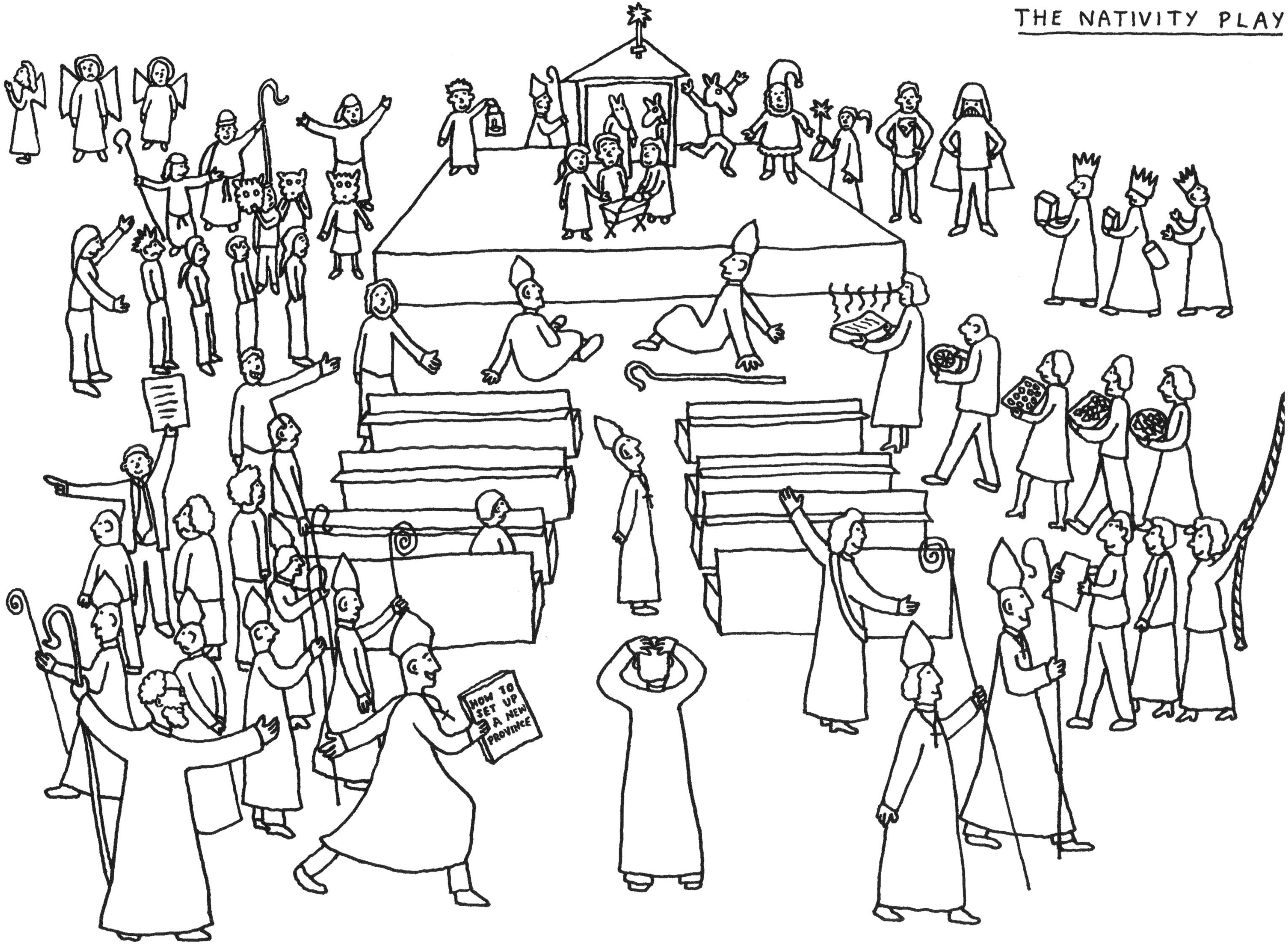
HOW TO SET UP A NEW PROVINCE

THE PCC GOES SHOPPING

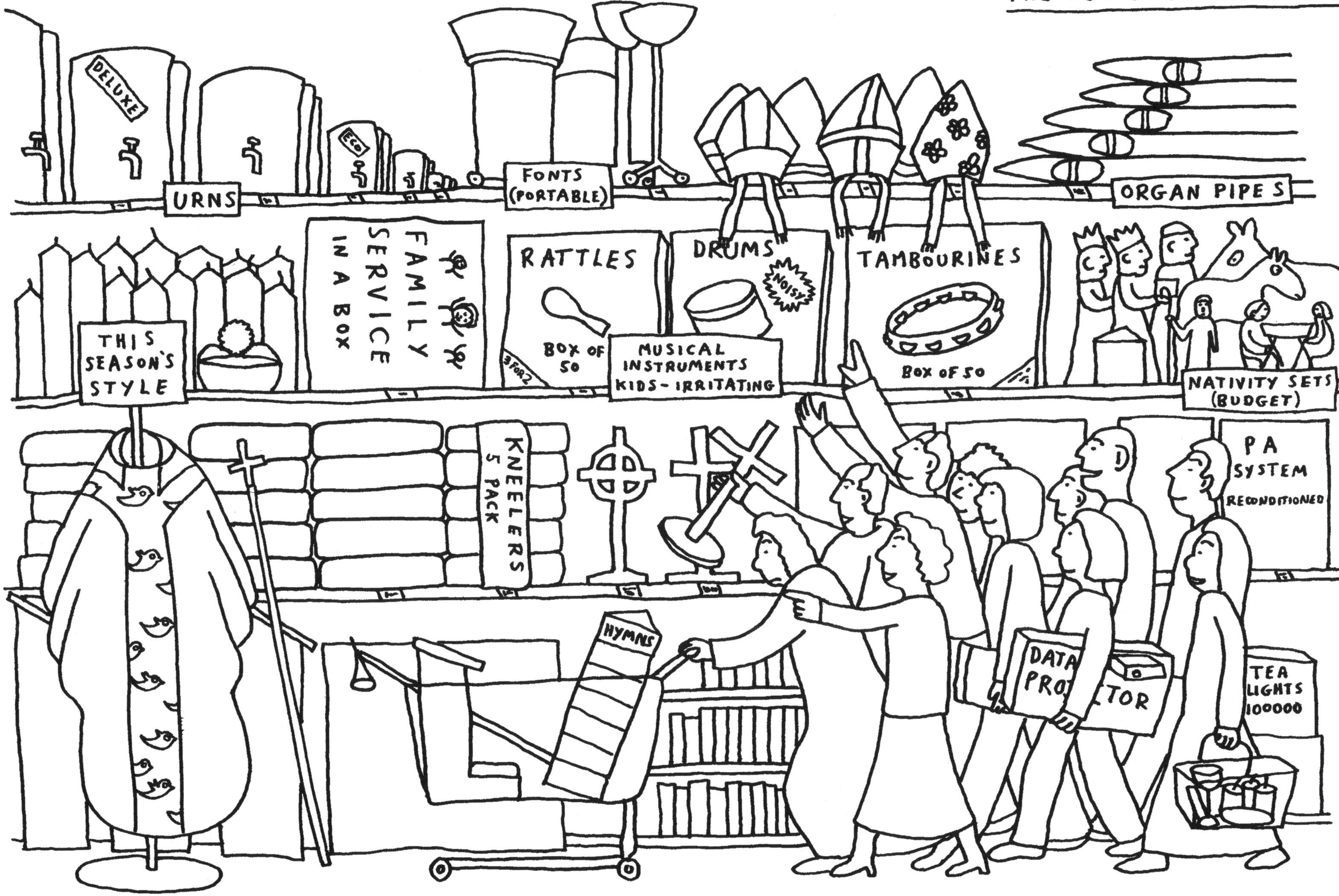
URNS
DELUXE
ECO
FONTS (PORTABLE)
ORGAN PIPES
THIS SEASON'S STYLE
FAMILY SERVICE IN A BOX
RATTLES
BOX OF 50
3 FOR 2
DRUMS
NOISY
MUSICAL INSTRUMENTS KIDS - IRRITATING
TAMBOURINES
BOX OF 50
NATIVITY SETS (BUDGET)
KNEELERS 5 PACK
HYMNS
PA SYSTEM RECONDITIONED
DATA PROJECTOR
TEA LIGHTS 100000

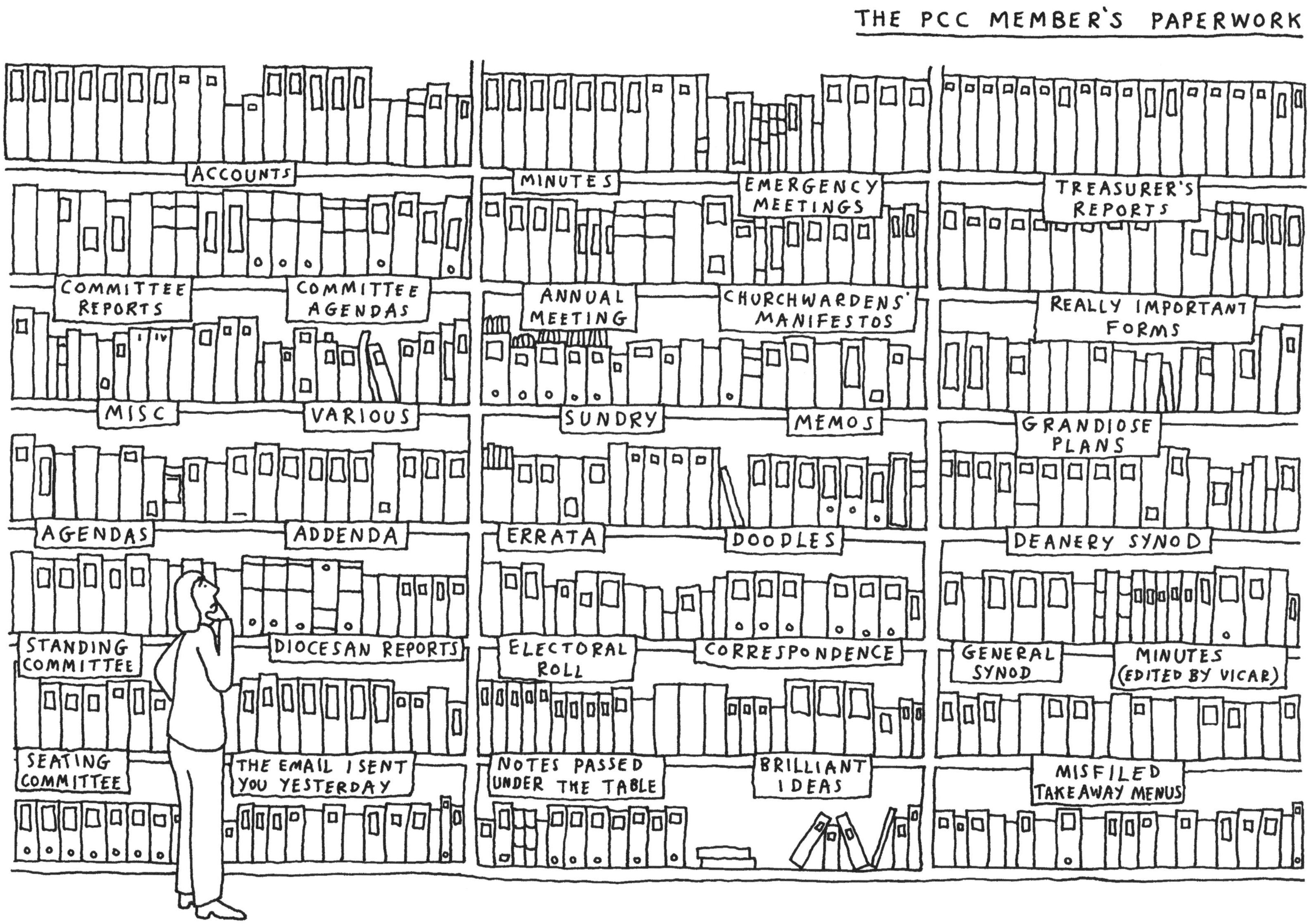
THE PCC MEMBER'S PAPERWORK
ACCOUNTS
MINUTES
EMERGENCY MEETINGS
TREASURER'S REPORTS
COMMITTEE REPORTS
COMMITTEE AGENDAS
ANNUAL MEETING
CHURCHWARDENS' MANIFESTOS
REALLY IMPORTANT FORMS
MISC
VARIOUS
SUNDRY
MEMOS
GRANDIOSE PLANS
AGENDAS
ADDENDA
ERRATA
DOODLES
DEANERY SYNOD
STANDING COMMITTEE
DIOCESAN REPORTS
ELECTORAL ROLL
CORRESPONDENCE
GENERAL SYNOD
MINUTES (EDITED BY VICAR)
SEATING COMMITTEE
THE EMAIL I SENT YOU YESTERDAY
NOTES PASSED UNDER THE TABLE
BRILLIANT IDEAS
MISFILED TAKEAWAY MENUS

THE PEACE

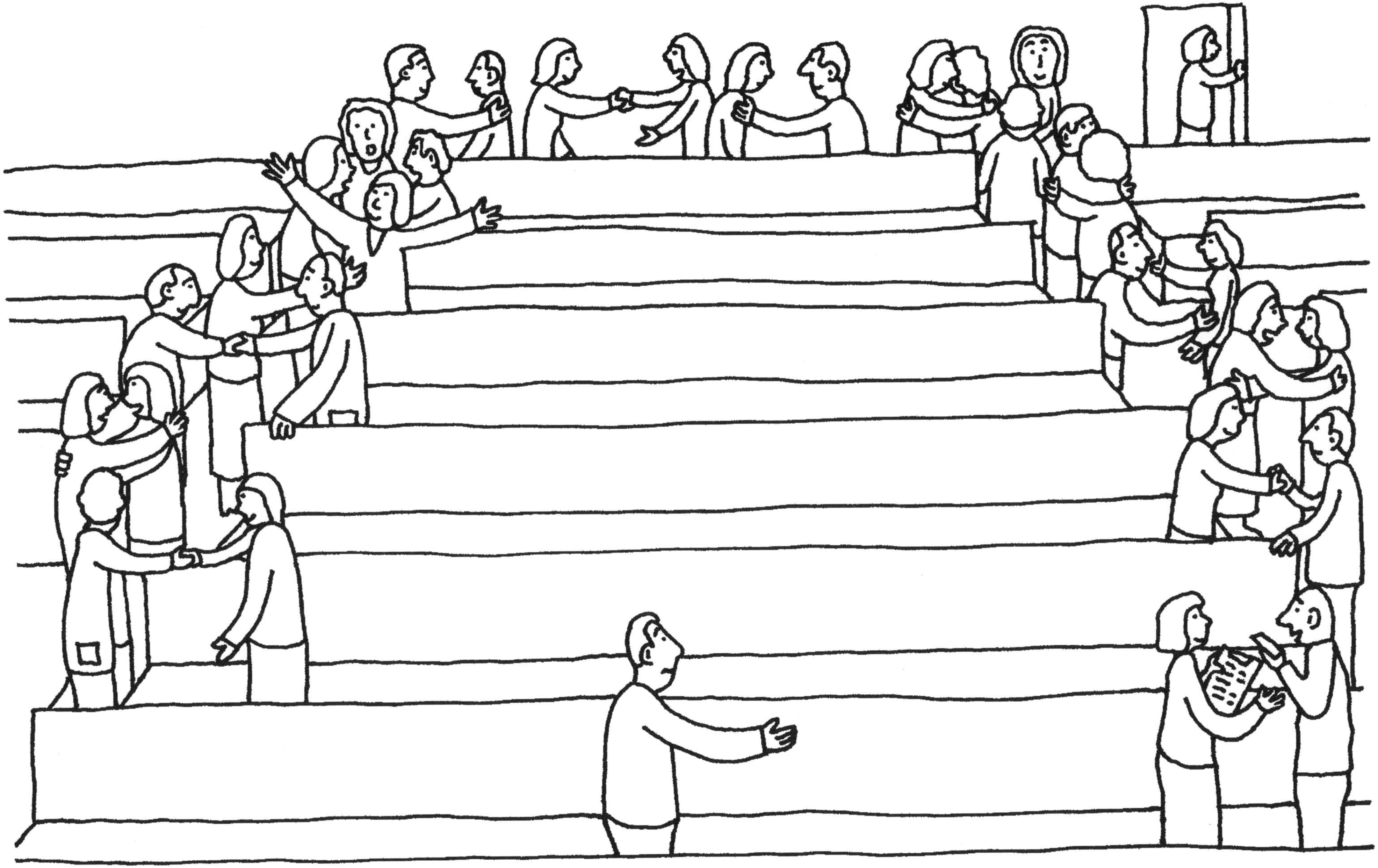

QUIZ NIGHT

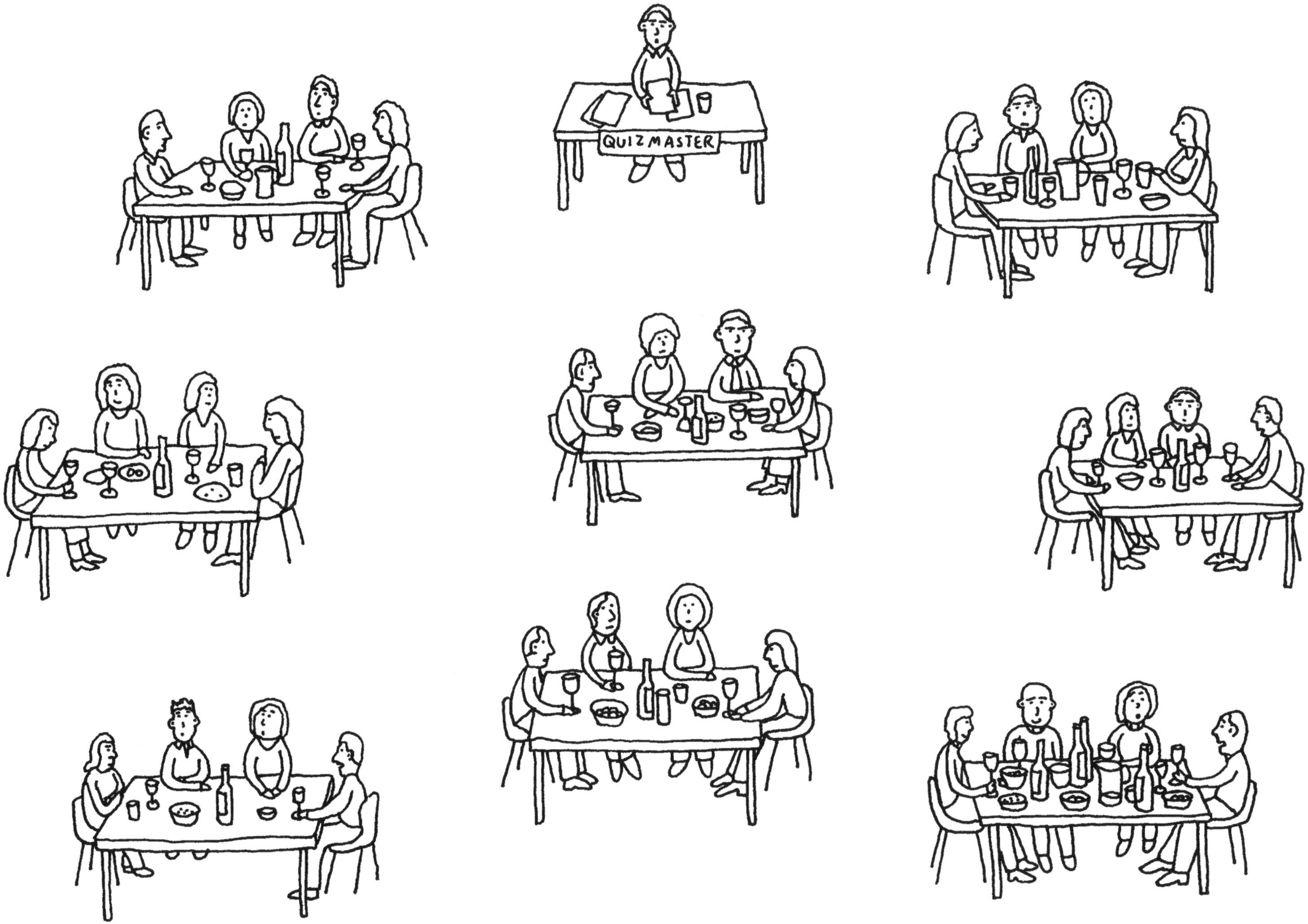
QUIZMASTER

THE SERMON ILLUSTRATION LENDING LIBRARY

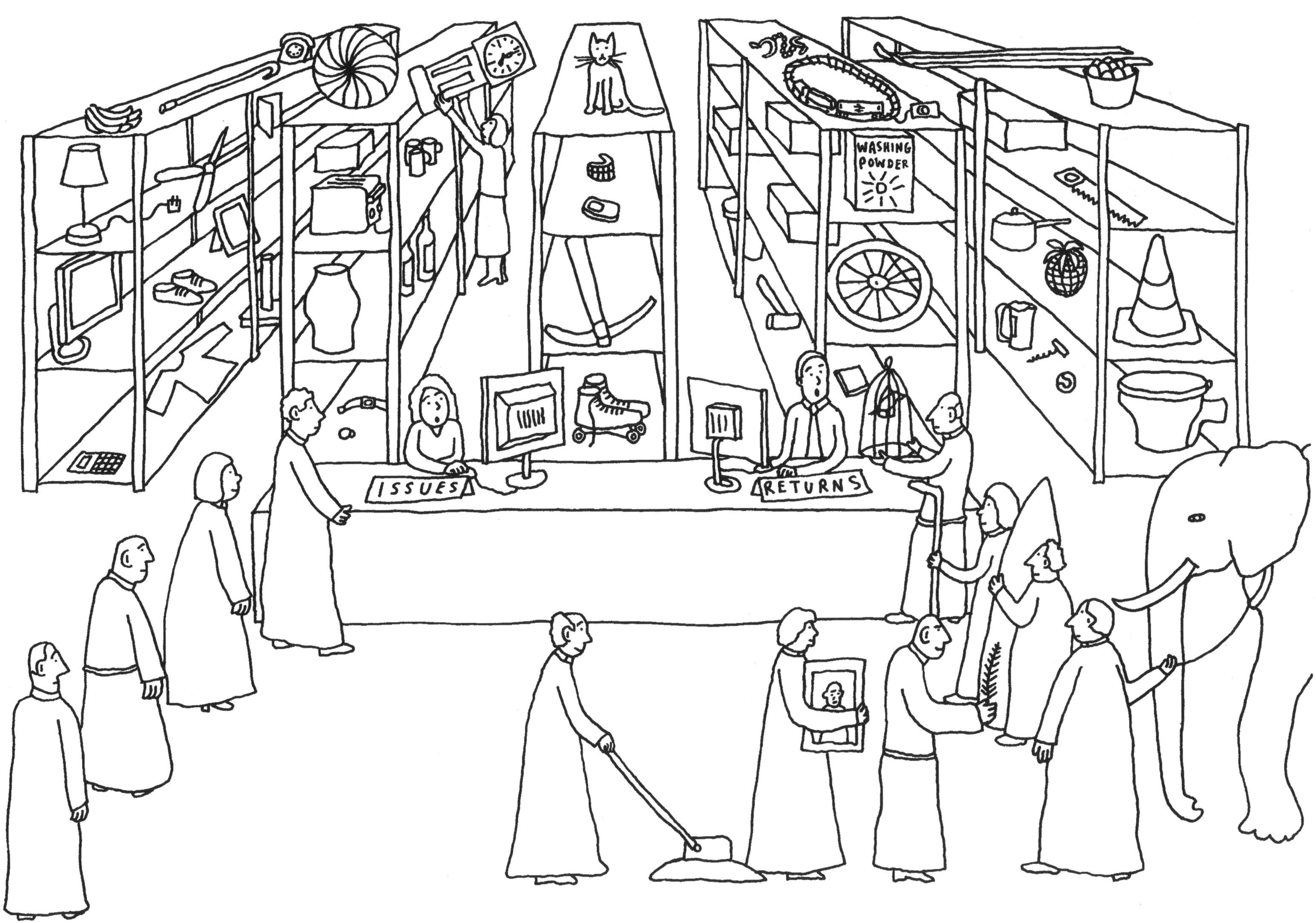

WASHING POWDER
ISSUES
RETURNS

SPRING CLEANING

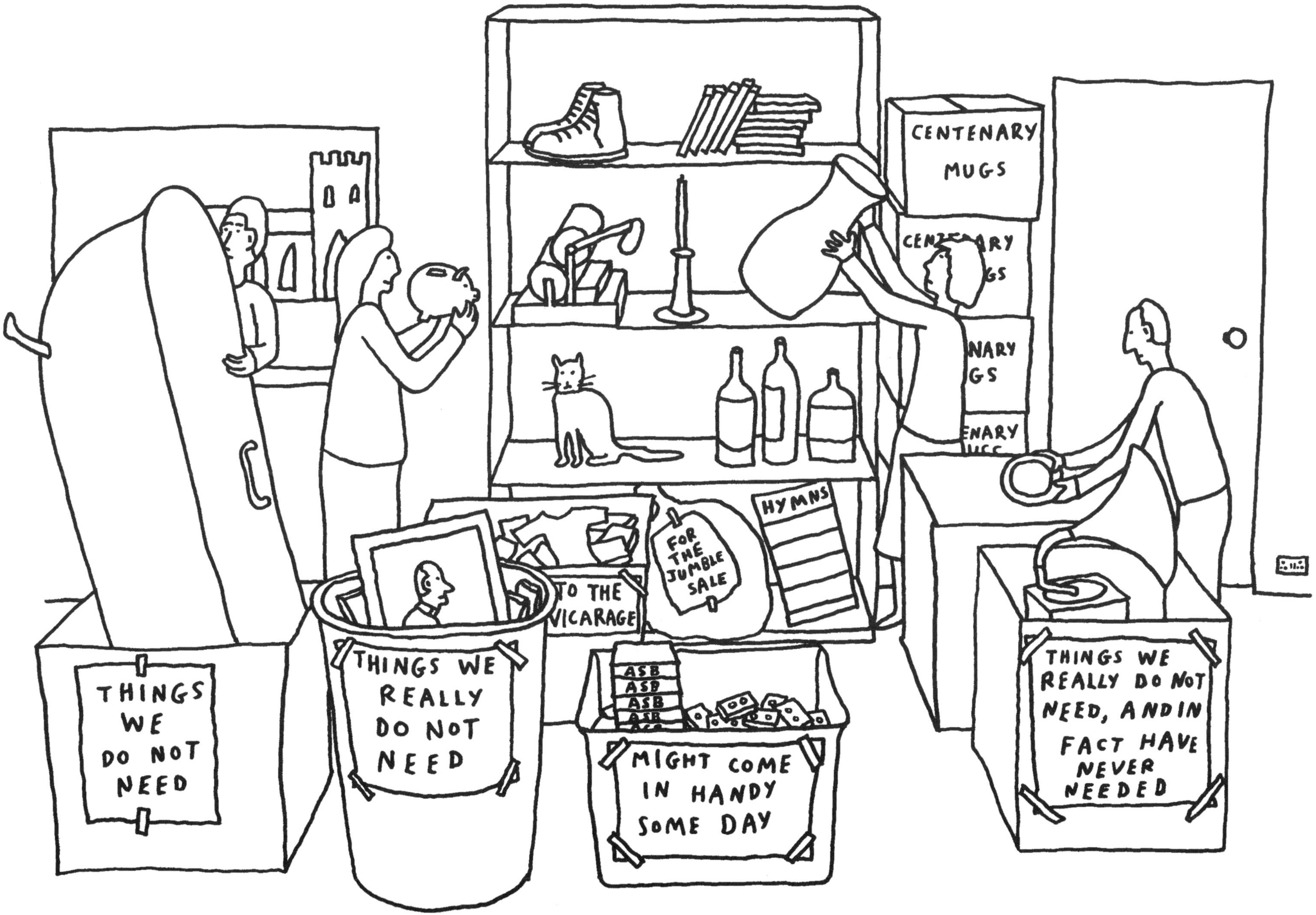
CENTENARY MUGS
HYMNS
FOR THE JUMBLE SALE
TO THE VICARAGE
ASB
THINGS WE DO NOT NEED
THINGS WE REALLY DO NOT NEED
MIGHT COME IN HANDY SOME DAY
THINGS WE REALLY DO NOT NEED, AND IN FACT HAVE NEVER NEEDED

THE SUNDAY SCHOOL

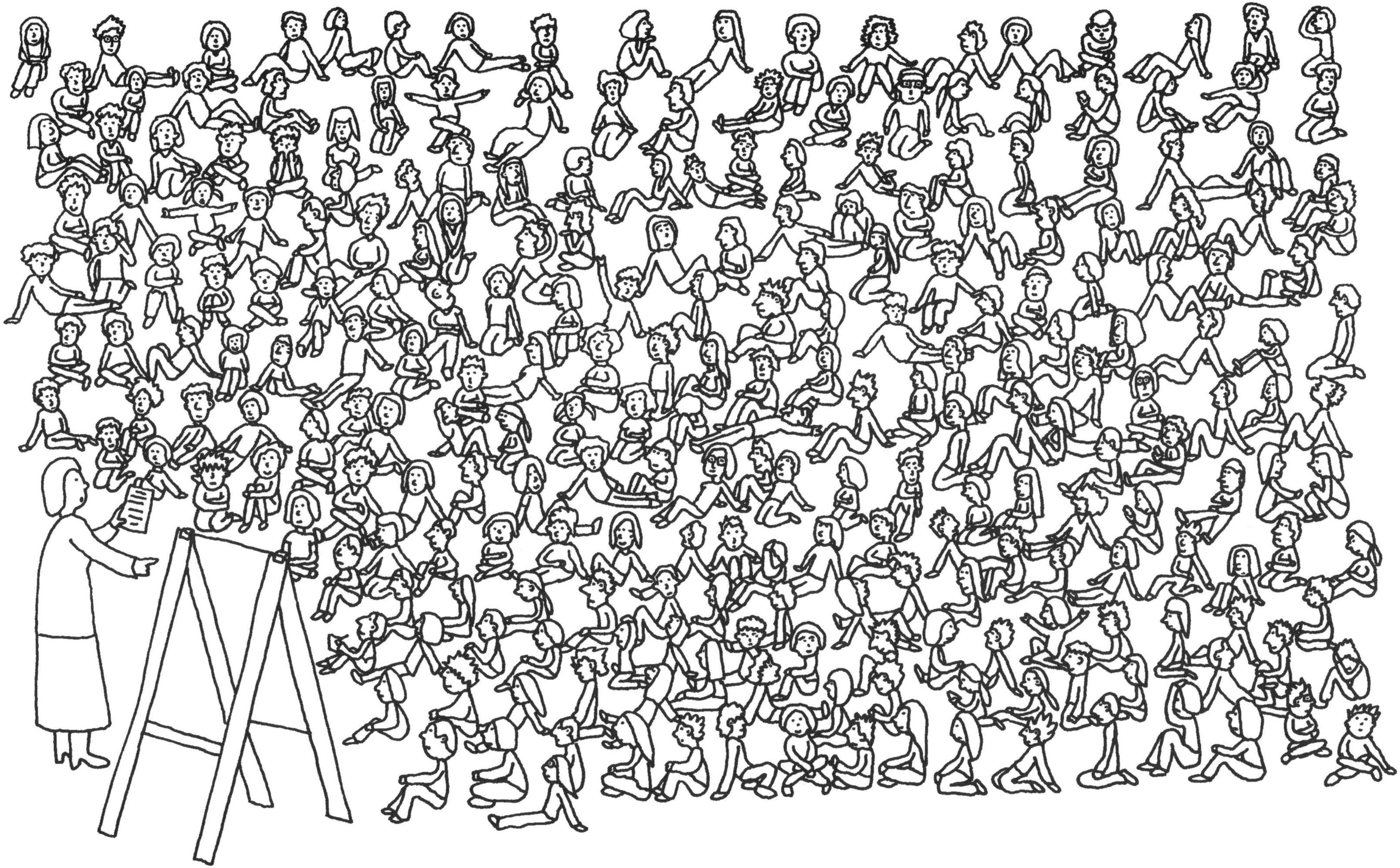

THE FLOWER ROTA

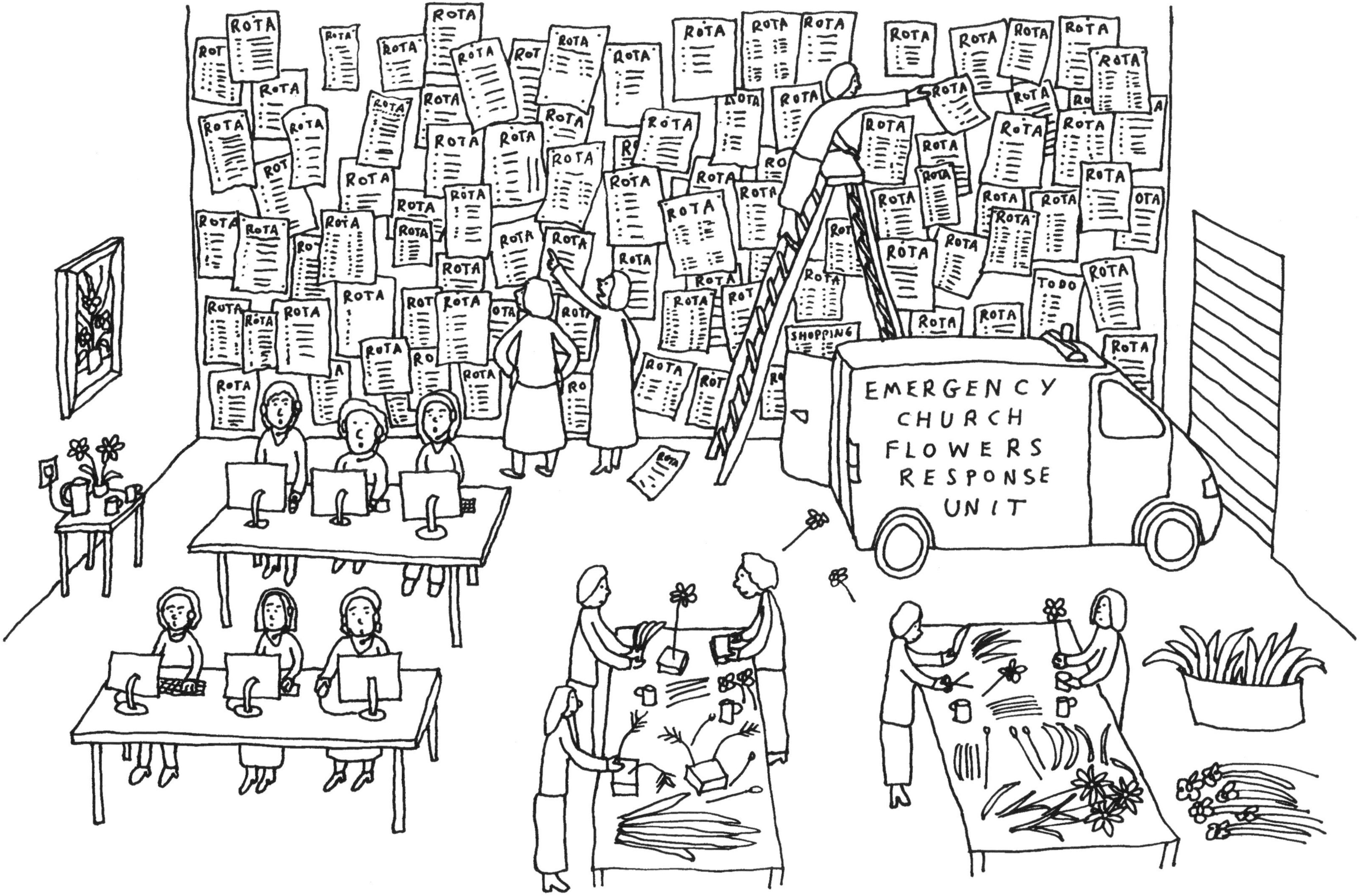

THE TODDLER GROUP

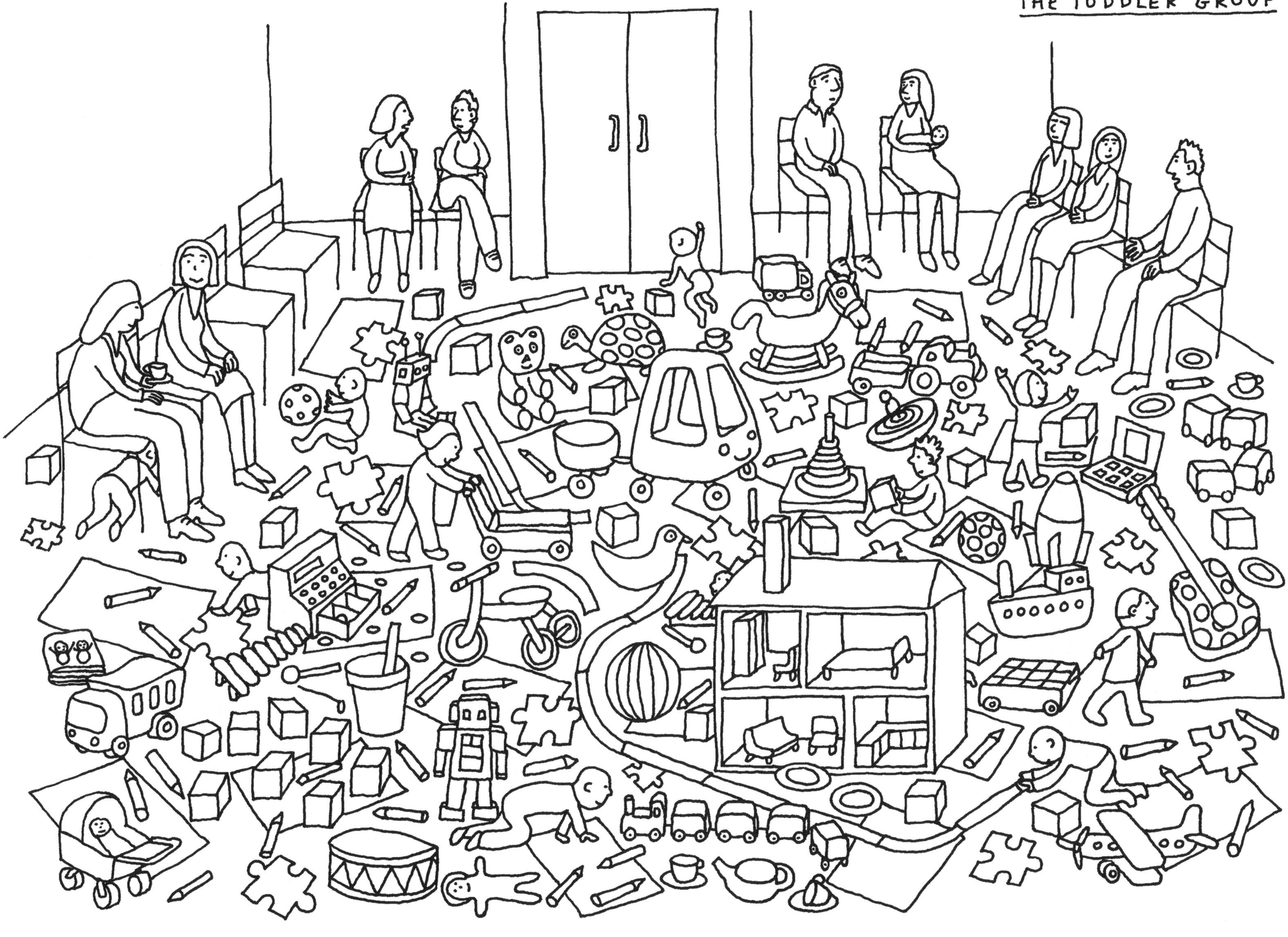

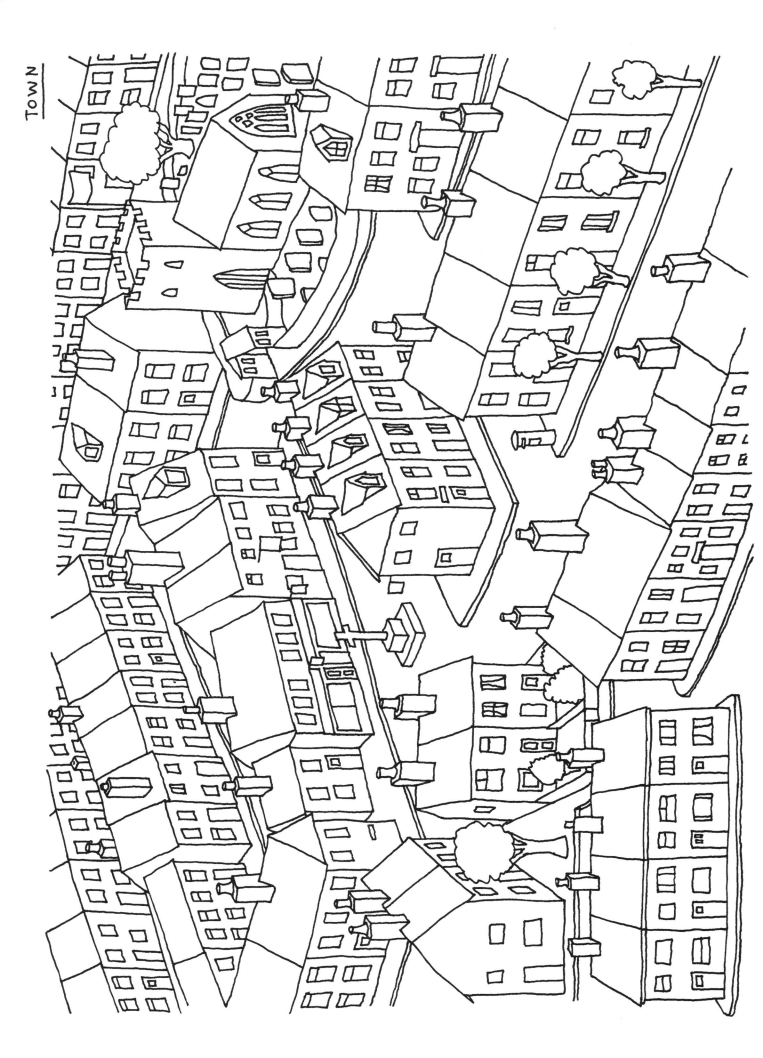

Town

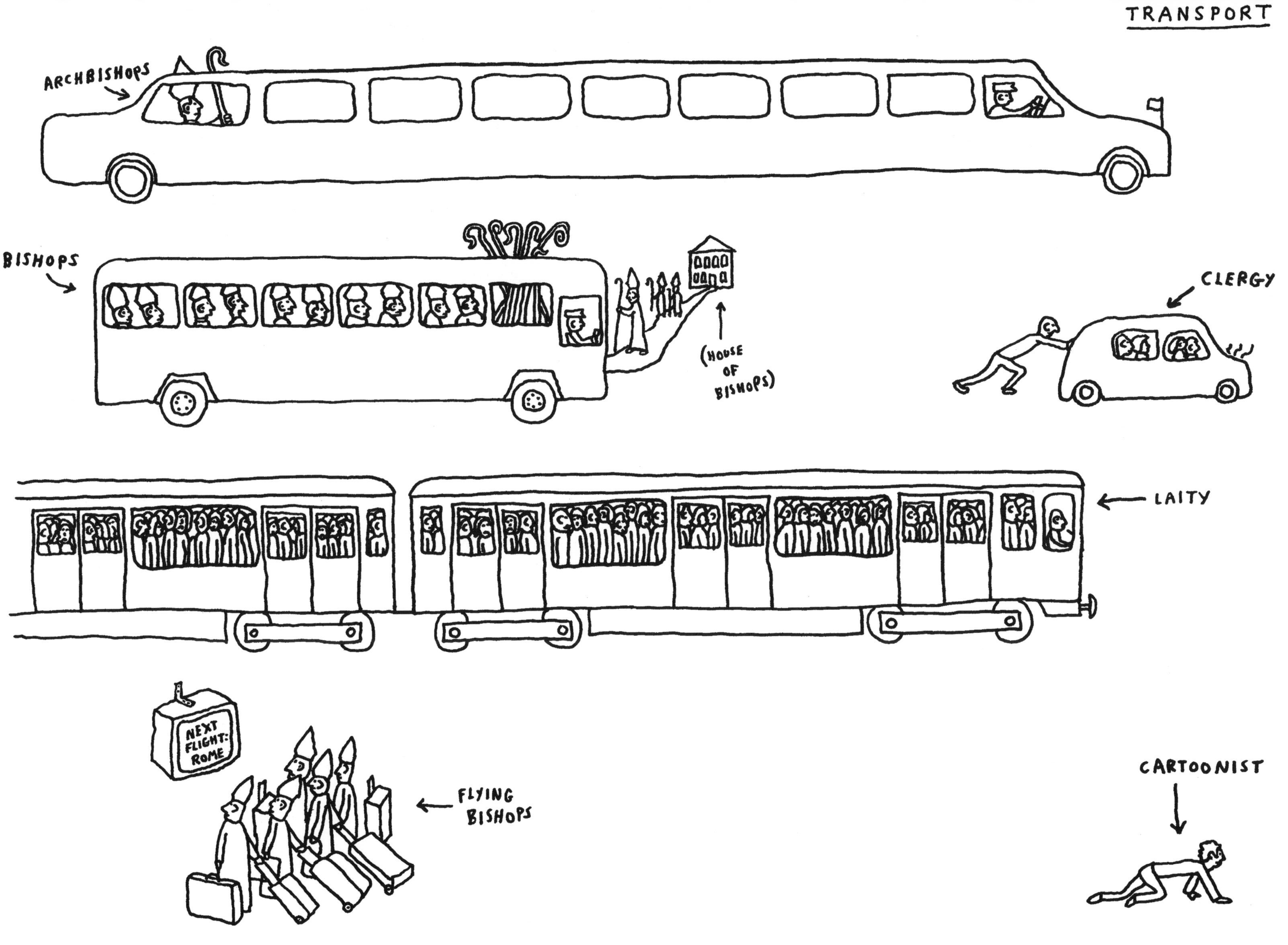
TRANSPORT
ARCHBISHOPS
BISHOPS
(HOUSE OF BISHOPS)
CLERGY
LAITY
NEXT FLIGHT: ROME
FLYING BISHOPS
CARTOONIST

THE VERGER'S STORE CUPBOARD

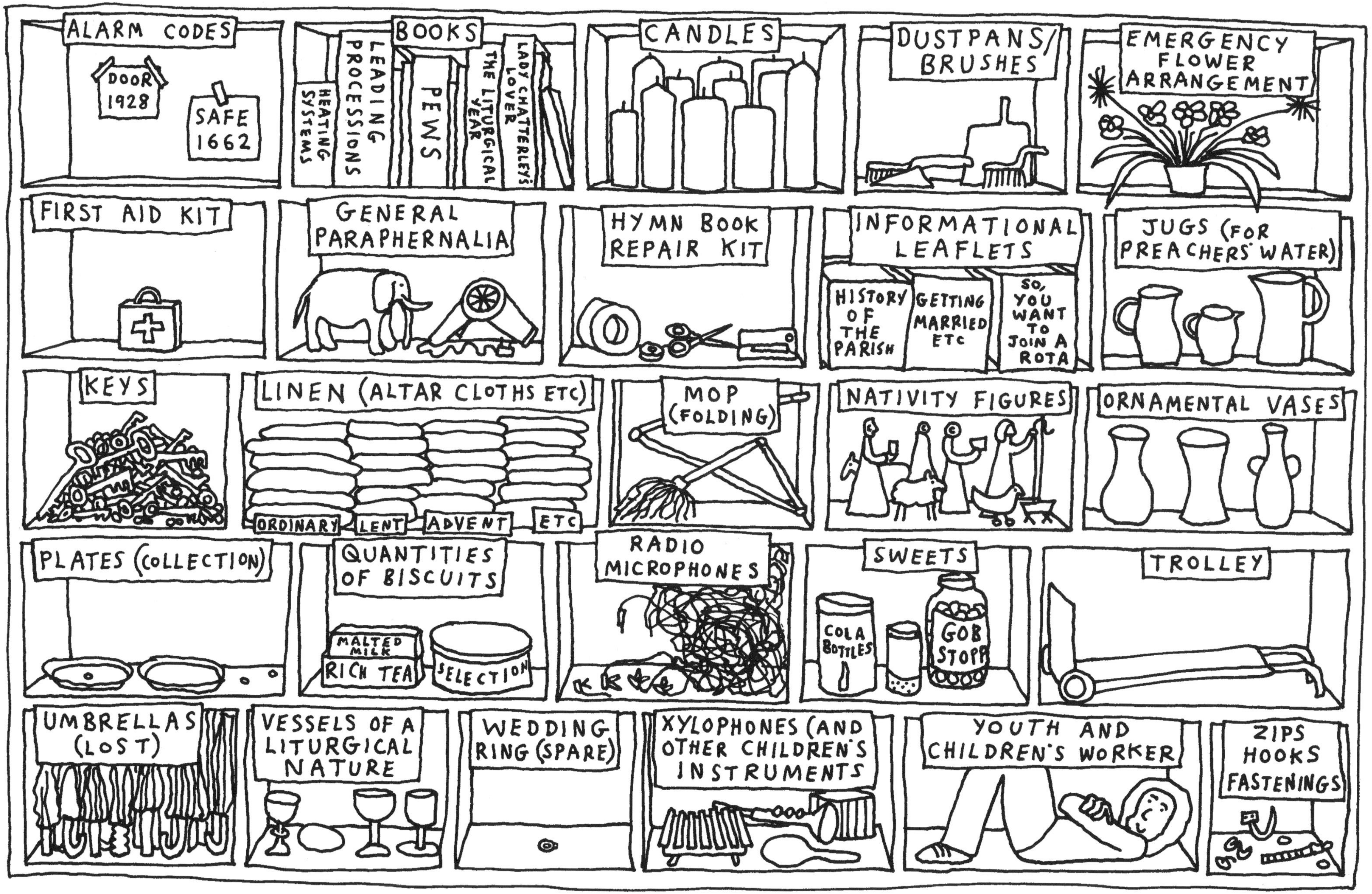
ALARM CODES
DOOR 1928
SAFE 1662
BOOKS
HEATING SYSTEMS
LEADING PROCESSIONS
PEWS
THE LITURGICAL YEAR
LADY CHATTERLEY'S LOVER
CANDLES
DUSTPANS/ BRUSHES
EMERGENCY FLOWER ARRANGEMENT
FIRST AID KIT
GENERAL PARAPHERNALIA
HYMN BOOK REPAIR KIT
INFORMATIONAL LEAFLETS
HISTORY OF THE PARISH
GETTING MARRIED ETC
SO, YOU WANT TO JOIN A ROTA
JUGS (FOR PREACHERS' WATER)
KEYS
LINEN (ALTAR CLOTHS ETC)
ORDINARY
LENT
ADVENT
ETC
MOP (FOLDING)
NATIVITY FIGURES
ORNAMENTAL VASES
PLATES (COLLECTION)
QUANTITIES OF BISCUITS
MALTED MILK
RICH TEA
SELECTION
RADIO MICROPHONES
SWEETS
COLA BOTTLES
GOB STOPP
TROLLEY
UMBRELLAS (LOST)
VESSELS OF A LITURGICAL NATURE
WEDDING RING (SPARE)
XYLOPHONES (AND OTHER CHILDREN'S INSTRUMENTS
YOUTH AND CHILDREN'S WORKER
ZIPS HOOKS FASTENINGS

THE WEDDING

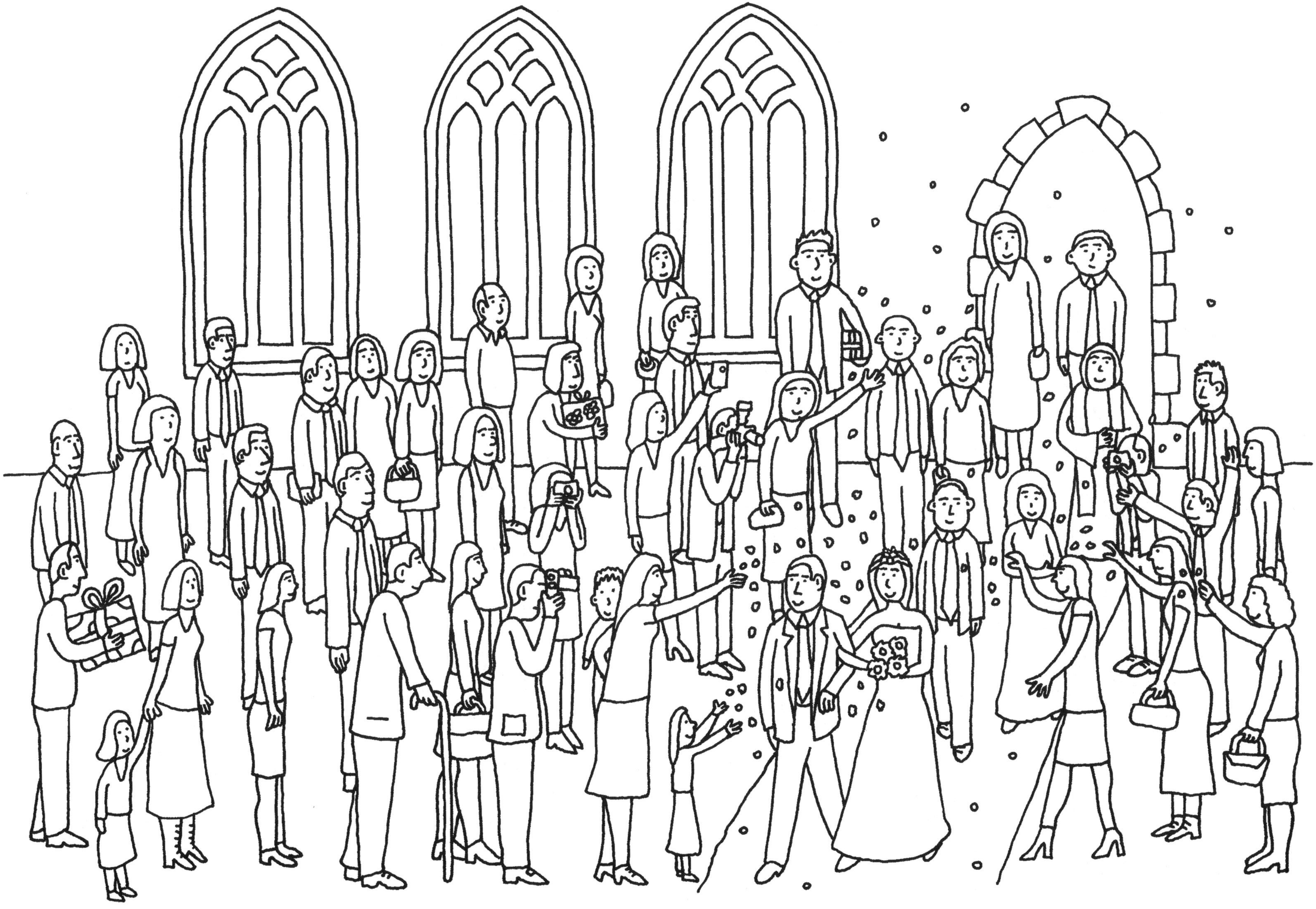

WHO IS LEADING US?

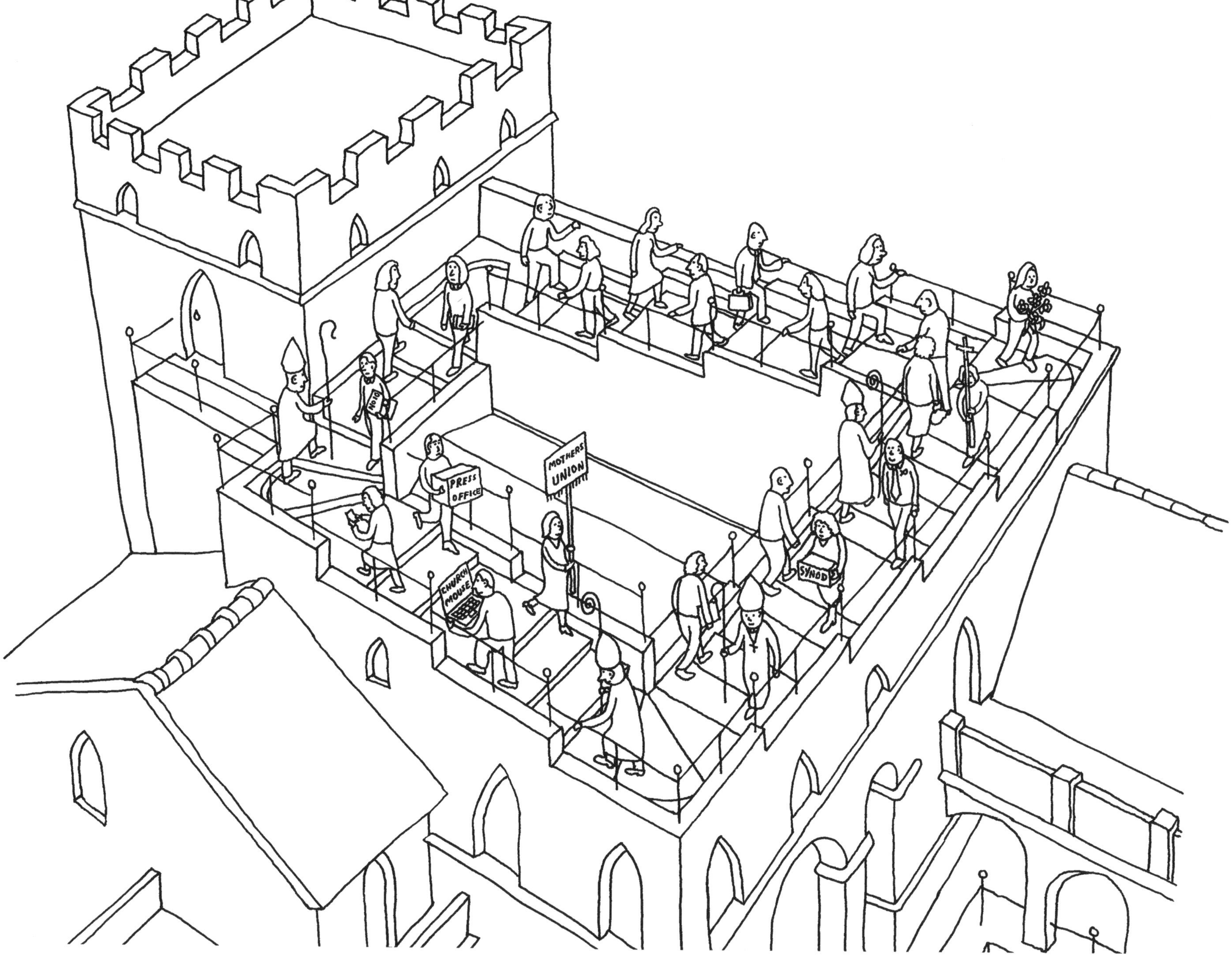

NOIO
PRESS OFFICE
MOTHERS UNION
CHURCH MOUSE
SYNOD

THE CHURCH THAT MEETS IN A SCHOOL HALL

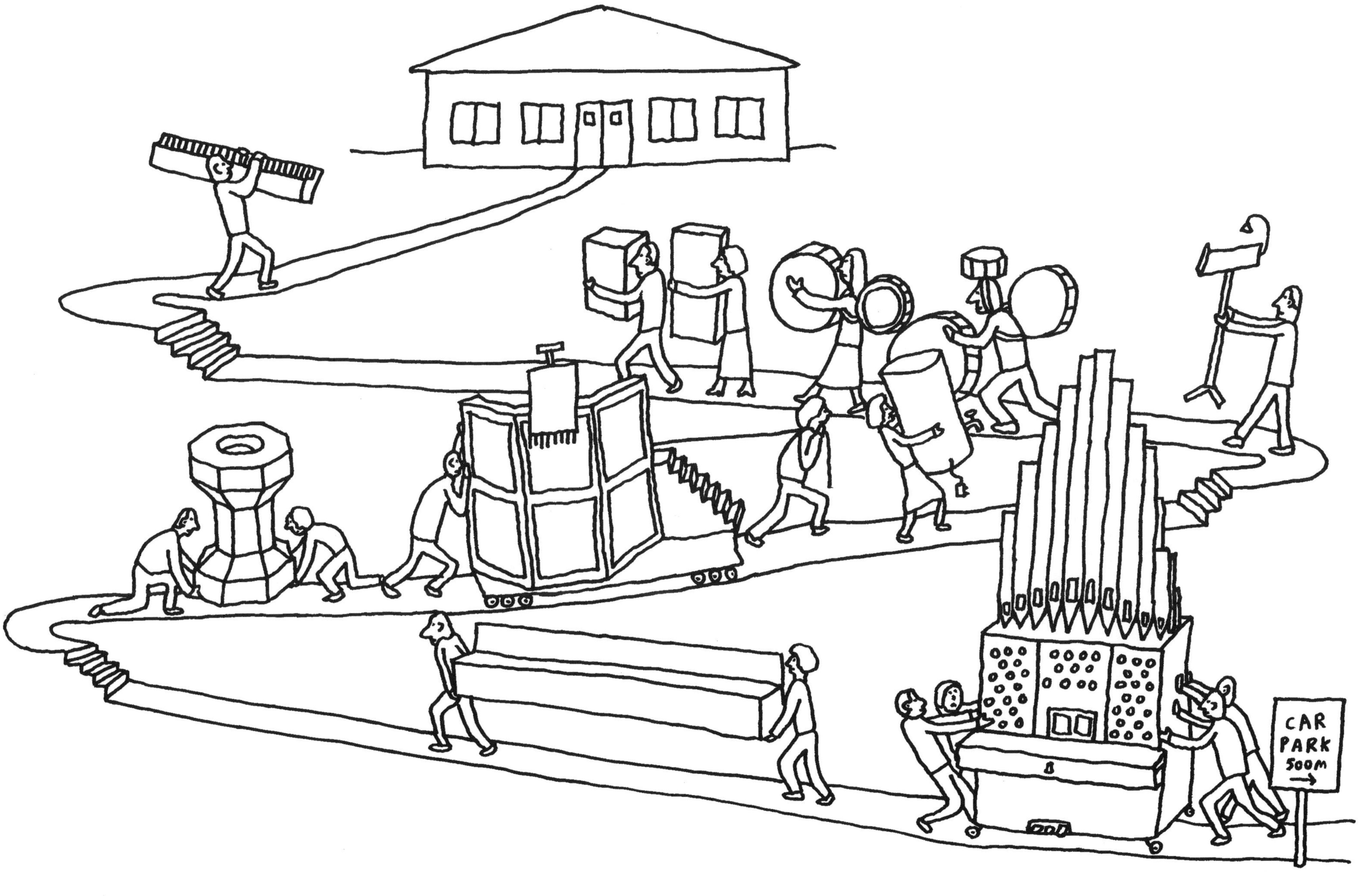
CAR
PARK
500m

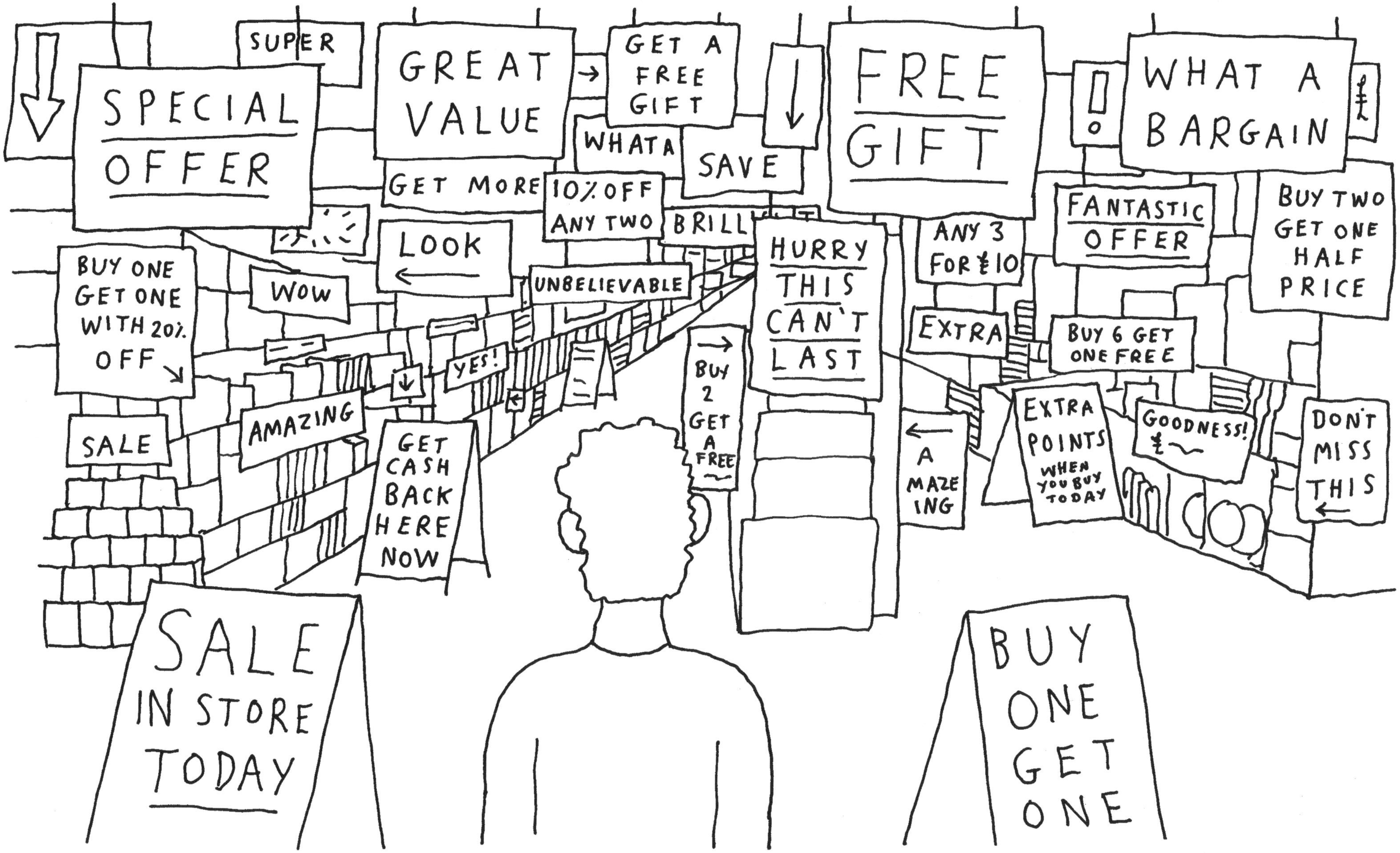
SUPER
SPECIAL OFFER
GREAT VALUE
GET A FREE GIFT
FREE GIFT
WHAT A BARGAIN
WHATA
SAVE
GET MORE
10% OFF ANY TWO
BRILL
FANTASTIC OFFER
BUY TWO GET ONE HALF PRICE
ANY 3 FOR £10
LOOK
BUY ONE GET ONE WITH 20% OFF
WOW
UNBELIEVABLE
HURRY THIS CAN'T LAST
EXTRA
BUY 6 GET ONE FREE
YES!
BUY 2 GET A FREE
SALE
AMAZING
GET CASH BACK HERE NOW
A MAZE ING
EXTRA POINTS WHEN YOU BUY TODAY
GOODNESS!
DON'T MISS THIS
SALE IN STORE TODAY
BUY ONE GET ONE

FLOWER ARRANGING

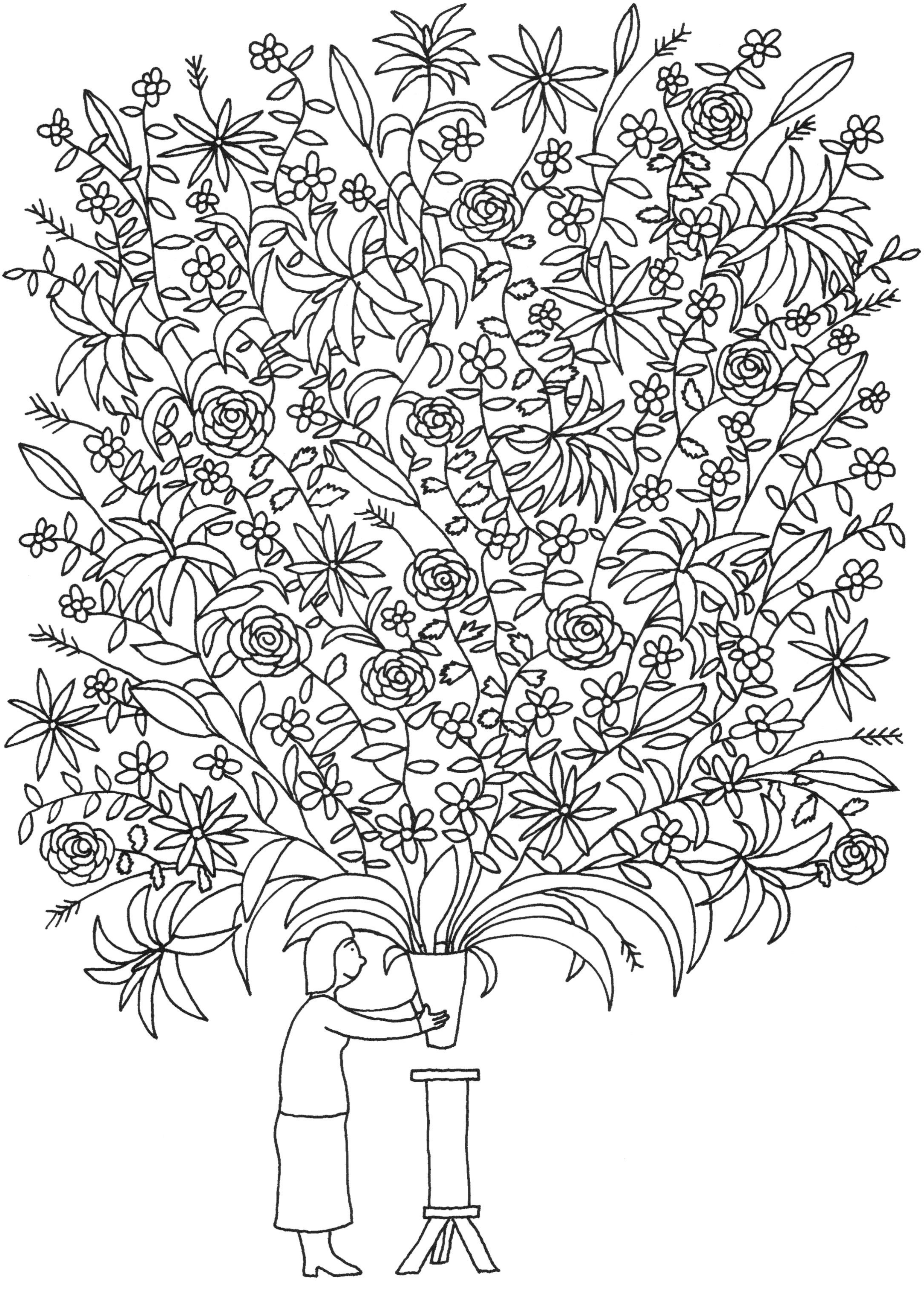